REPRESENTATIVE AMERICAN SPEECHES 1976-1977

edited by WALDO W. BRADEN
Boyd Professor of Speech
Louisiana State University

THE REFERENCE SHELF
Volume 49   Number 4

D0067779

THE H. W. WILSON COMPANY
New York   1977

815.
R

THE REFERENCE SHELF

The books in this series contain reprints of articles, excerpts from books, and addresses on current issues and social trends in the United States and other countries. There are six separately bound numbers in each volume, all of which are generally published in the same calendar year. One number is a collection of recent speeches; each of the others is devoted to a single subject and gives background information and discussion from various points of view, concluding with a comprehensive bibliography. Books in the series may be purchased individually or on subscription.

Library of Congress Catalog Card
Representative American speeches, 1937/38–
    New York, H. W. Wilson Co.
        v. 21. cm. annual. (The Reference shelf)
    Editors: 1937/38–1958/59, A. C. Baird.–1959/60–1969/70,
        L. Thonssen.–1970/71–   W. W. Braden.

    I. American orations.   2. Speeches, addresses, etc.
I. Baird, Albert Craig, ed.   II. Thonssen, Lester,
ed.   III. Braden, Waldo W., ed.   IV. Series.
PS668.B3   815.5082   38–27962

100346
c.2

PREFACE

AN OVERVIEW OF PUBLIC ADDRESS, 1976-1977

In the fall of 1976 the Library of Congress opened an exhibition of landmarks in the exploration of ideas and places that it called "Beginnings." Introducing this event, Daniel J. Boorstin, the Librarian of Congress, wrote "Great beginnings dramatize our power of renewal. . . . The USA has been the land of new beginnings." Similar thoughts were expressed by President Jimmy Carter when he spoke of "a new beginning, a new dedication within our government, and a new spirit among us all," in his inaugural address. These statements suggest the theme and mood of many of the speeches in REPRESENTATIVE AMERICAN SPEECHES: 1976–1977—a reflection of the spirit of beginning, of what Archibald MacLeish has called promises.

The two political conventions, the nation's Bicentennial, the campaign, the presidential debates, the inauguration of the new president, the beginning of a new Administration offered Americans an unusual amount and variety of public speaking, or as some would say, in a disparaging tone, "oratory."

Throughout the year the politicians, as always, produced the greatest quantities (and possibly the least quality) of public speaking. After hard-fought primaries each party narrowed its choice to two or three persons (at a total cost of almost 78 million dollars) and then assembled in national conventions: the Democrats in Madison Square Garden in New York City and the Republicans at Kemper Arena in Kansas City, Missouri. Little of the speaking that occurred at these two carefully staged media events could qualify as stirring or eloquent. Fred M. Hechinger (New York *Times*, August 24, 1976) analyzed the "noisy hoopla and purple rhetoric" in the observation: "What the conventions pro-

3

vide is a few hours of the illusion of participatory democracy, with plenty of free TV exposure to the folks at home."

During the fall political campaigns Gerald Ford and Jimmy Carter took center stage. The season's offering included three presidential debates, a vice presidential debate, and many sideshows among which were two particularly vigorous contests for seats in the United States Senate. In California, Dr. S. I. Hayakawa (conservative Republican), professor, college president emeritus, and semanticist, won over incumbent John V. Tunney (liberal Democrat). In New York State, Daniel Patrick Moynihan (Democrat), an intermittent Harvard professor, defeated incumbent James Buckley (Republican-Conservative). Through the results of these two elections, each party gained a senator who is capable of significant speaking.

Looking at the presidential campaign as a whole, reporters often expressed their disgust with what they observed. Alan L. Otten (*Wall Street Journal*, October 21, 1976) spoke of the "emptiness and dreariness of the campaign." Tom Wicker (New York *Times*, October 24, 1976) called it "the most trivial and vituperative—in memory." Arthur Schlesinger Jr. said that "no campaign within memory has collapsed into such shameful triviality" (*Wall Street Journal*, November 1, 1976). John Chancellor of NBC reported that in more than twenty years he had not seen "a pettier . . . emptier campaign . . . so lacking in a discussion of real issues" (New York *Times*, October 25, 1976). James Reston concluded that Ford and Carter had "loitered down into an increasingly trivial and even nasty argument over secondary issues, and . . . contributed to the cynicism . . . about the whole American political process." He thought that neither of them had "made a single noble or even memorable speech" (New York *Times*, October 15, 1976).

Most observers agree that President Jimmy Carter has brought a style to the public forum that contrasts favorably with that of the previous eight years. In office the President has had frequent press conferences, two Fireside Chats, a

live, televised, two-hour question-and-answer session with
the voters, and a nationally televised appearance at a New
England Town Meeting (at Clinton, Massachusetts). A headline in the *Christian Science Monitor* for April 28, 1977, declared, "Carter's style has many breathless." Richard L.
Strout went on to say that the President "shows every evidence of being a strong President. He shows political savvy.
Elected by a thin majority, he has successfully cultivated, in
a short time, sizable popular support by unusual use of
press, radio, television, and a series of image-creating symbols. . . . His determination to be a strong President is illustrated by willingness to spend some of his popularity on
difficult issues, like energy conservation." The reporters and
the voters have had trouble shifting from the imperial
Nixon to the populist Carter.

*   *   *

The publication of REPRESENTATIVE AMERICAN SPEECHES:
1976-1977 marks the fortieth anniversary of a series that
started with the 1937-1938 number. Since that time the years
have been filled with dramatic events that have produced
many examples of rhetoric and eloquence. With kaleido-
scopic variety the compilations run through ten presidential elections, World War II, the formation of the United
Nations, Korea, Vietnam, the launching of Sputnik, the as-
sassinations of John F. Kennedy, Martin Luther King Jr.,
and Robert F. Kennedy, space voyages to the moon, Vietnam protests and riots of the late sixties, the 1974 oil embargo, Watergate, the resignation of President Richard M.
Nixon, and finally the Bicentennial.

In these forty years the three editors, A. Craig Baird
(1938-1959), Lester Thonssen (1960-1970), the present editor (since 1971), have been privileged to study closely the
words of many orators who have significantly influenced
American thought and policies. Since 1937 the editors have
perused well over five thousand speeches and have chosen
some eight hundred made by about five hundred different

speakers. They have turned to forty speakers more than once. Leading the list of those represented by more than one speech have been Franklin D. Roosevelt with twenty-three speeches and Dwight D. Eisenhower with twenty-one. Political figures have received more space than any other group because they resort more often to speechmaking in the course of their business. On the other hand, many selections were by speakers from diverse fields, among whom were Douglas MacArthur (soldier), William Norwood Brigance (speech educator), James B. Conant (scientist), Harry Emerson Fosdick (minister), Virginius Dabney (editor and historian), René J. Dubos (scientist), Theodore M. Hesburgh (educator), Walter Lippmann (journalist), Robert M. Hutchins (educator), Martin Luther King Jr. (civil rights leader), Edward R. Murrow (radio commentator), Margaret Mead (anthropologist), Reinhold Niebuhr (theologian), Arthur Schlesinger Jr. (historian), and Glenn T. Seaborg (scientist).

Speeches of visitors from other countries have rarely been included, but the editors did make exceptions for Edward Beneš, Winston Churchill, Anthony Eden, Madame Chang Kai-shek, C. P. Snow, Charles H. Malik, Pope Paul VI, and Arnold J. Toynbee.

A fitting memory for this section is a statement that Lester Thonssen wrote for the introduction to REPRESENTATIVE AMERICAN SPEECHES: 1965-1966.

J. Donald Adams, retired editor of the New York *Times Book Review*, once remarked that "words are almost on a par with the weather in their universality of appeal." Reflecting on the use and abuse of our common tongue, he said that "words remain one of the most living things of man's creation; indeed, one might argue that they have more vitality than anything else we have fashioned." The measure of their vitality and power has varied from age to age. So has the recognition of verbal competence as a standard of a man's worth. In the area of public address, for example, we continue to speculate whether high skill in speaking is a requirement for effective leadership. Must the public man be an orator? Is oratory influential in our time? . . . Reporter Tom Wicker of the New York *Times*, conceding that eloquence and greatness in public figures were not the same, yet concluded that "in politics the former is almost always the indispensable tool of the latter." The noted French author André Maurois went even further, declaring that "the worth of a statesman's character is often equivalent to the excellence of his prose."

Frequently the editors have been asked, What are the best places to find speeches? Day in and day out the *Congressional Record* prints more speeches than any other source. In addition to their own speaking (much of it pedestrian) in the nation's legislative halls, congressmen read into the *Record* a never-ending variety of material including speeches of others. The New York *Times* and *Vital Speeches of the Day* are also fruitful sources. Friends and colleagues of the editors have often provided helpful tips on items to be considered. The editors have always welcomed as much help as possible from these sources.

Many persons have generously contributed to this book. The speakers and their aides have willingly supplied texts and background materials. As always, Clinton Bradford, Stephen Cooper, Ronald Garay, Mary Frances Hopkins, Francine Merritt, Harold Mixon and Owen Peterson have offered much needed counsel. Valuable suggestions were forwarded to me by Mary Margaret Roberts of Kansas State College of Pittsburg, Ruth Arrington of Northeast Oklahoma State University, Cal Logue of the University of Georgia, and David Cornell of Wittenberg University, Springfield, Ohio. Lester Thonssen, the former editor, has given me much needed advice. John Pennybacker, my departmental chairman, has been supportive in the whole project, as indeed have many of my colleagues at Louisiana State University. Of course the volume could not have been completed without the hard work of my secretary, Virginia Steely. I have been most fortunate to have had the friendship and assistance of these persons and many others.

WALDO W. BRADEN

July 1977
Baton Rouge, Louisiana

CONTENTS

PREFACE: An Overview of Public Address, 1976–1977   3

A NEW BEGINNING: A NEW DEDICATION

Barbara Jordan. Keynote Address   11
Jimmy Carter. The Inaugural Address   18
Paul Moore Jr. A Biblical Faith for a President   24

DEMOCRACY IN ACTION

Gerald R. Ford—Jimmy Carter. The Third Presidential
    Debate   30
Julian Goodman. Broadcast Journalism: Serving the
    Democratic Process   52
Lowell Weicker Jr. Televised Debates   61

IN PURSUIT OF EQUALITY

Eleanor Holmes Norton. In Pursuit of Equality in
    Academe: New Themes and Dissonant Chords   65
Elizabeth Holtzman. Women and Equality Under the
    Law   80

SOLUTIONS TO MALNUTRITION AND SQUALOR

Robert S. McNamara. Searching for New Solutions to
    Poverty   91
John A. Hannah. Meeting World Food Needs   103

CHOICES FOR THE FUTURE

Jimmy Carter. Energy Problems 117
Cyrus R. Vance. Human Rights and the Foreign Policy 127

OF MIND AND SPIRIT

Daniel J. Boorstin. Beginnings 138
Sol M. Linowitz. "Let Candles Be Brought" 149
Glenn A. Crosby. The Uses of Adversity 156
Krister Stendahl. "Faith That Enlivens the Mind" .. 168
Wallace A. Bacon. Language and the Lived World ... 174

FOR FREEDOM'S BIRTHDAY

Francis B. Sayre Jr. The Tall Ships 181
Bicentennial of American Independence 185
   Warren E. Burger 186
   Carl Albert 188
   Nelson A. Rockefeller 190
   Gerald R. Ford 192

APPENDIX: Biographical Notes 197

CUMULATIVE AUTHOR INDEX: 1970–1971 — 1976–1977 .. 204

A NEW BEGINNING: A NEW DEDICATION

KEYNOTE ADDRESS [1]

Barbara Jordan [2]

The Democrats had two keynote speakers at their national convention that met at Madison Square Garden in New York City, July 12-July 15, 1976: Senator John H. Glenn Jr. of Ohio, former astronaut, reported under consideration for the vice presidency, and Representative Barbara Jordan of Texas. Concerning the selection of Jordan, David E. Rosenbaum (New York *Times*, July 15, 1976) commented: "She was selected to give a keynote address . . . because she is black and a woman, but in part also because at age forty, she is one of the most prominent Democrats in the country, her color and gender notwithstanding." Jordan gave one of the best speeches presented at either of the national conventions.

The agenda presented the speaker with a difficult problem. When she started speaking at 11:50 P.M. almost four hours had elapsed since the session convened. The three thousand in attendance were wearied by a program that had already included the invocation, the presentation of the colors, appointment of the temporary chairman, the treasurer's report, the finance report, a convention film, and seven other speeches including the first keynote address. John Glenn's mundane effort had stirred little enthusiasm and some observers feel that his speech may have cost him the vice presidential nomination.

Taking command of the situation, Miss Jordan delivered a rousing ten-minute speech. In recognition of her own presence as a black woman elected to the House of Representatives, she observed in opening:

> One hundred and forty-four years ago, members of the Democratic party first met in convention to select a presidential candidate. . . . But there is something different about tonight. There is something special about tonight. What is different? What is special? I, Barbara Jordan, am a keynote speaker.
>
> A lot of years passed since 1832, and during that time it would have been most unusual for any national political

[1] Delivered to the National Democratic Convention meeting in Madison Square Garden, New York City, July 12, 1976. Quoted by permission.
[2] For biographical note, see Appendix.

party to ask that a Barbara Jordan deliver a keynote address . . . but tonight here I am. And I feel that notwithstanding the past, that my presence here is one additional bit of evidence that the American Dream need not forever be deferred.

She spoke with directness and force, seldom referring to her manuscript, which she preferred to a teleprompter. What she said reflected her deep convictions, her eagerness to address the convention, and her confidence that she reflected the sentiments of many Democrats. She is a forceful speaker with excellent control of pauses, contrasts, and emphasis of key ideas. She has a good voice, clear enunciation, an expressive face, and good posture. She leaves little doubt as to her control of the speaking situation.

She was one of the few speakers at either national convention to receive an immediate roar of approval that brought them back to the platform. David Brinkley of NBC commented: "For the first time, the convention has come alive. She is the star."

One hundred and forty-four years ago, members of the Democratic party first met in convention to select a presidential candidate. Since that time, Democrats have continued to convene once every four years and draft a party platform and nominate a presidential candidate. And our meeting this week is a continuation of that tradition.

But there is something different about tonight. There is something special about tonight. What is different? What is special? I, Barbara Jordan, am a keynote speaker.

A lot of years passed since 1832, and during that time it would have been most unusual for any national political party to ask that a Barbara Jordan deliver a keynote address . . . but tonight here I am. And I feel that notwithstanding the past that my presence here is one additional bit of evidence that the American Dream need not forever be deferred.

Now that I have this grand distinction what in the world am I supposed to say?

I could easily spend this time praising the accomplishments of this party and attacking the Republicans but I don't choose to do that.

I could list the many problems which Americans have. I could list the problems which cause people to feel cynical, angry, frustrated: problems which include lack of integrity in government; the feeling that the individual no longer counts; the reality of material and spiritual poverty; the feeling that the grand American experiment is failing or has failed. I could recite these problems and then I could sit down and offer no solutions. But I don't choose to do that either.

The citizens of America expect more. They deserve and they want more than a recital of problems.

We are a people in a quandary about the present. We are a people in search of our future. We are a people in search of a national community.

We are a people trying not only to solve the problems of the present: unemployment, inflation . . . but we are attempting on a larger scale to fulfill the promise of America. We are attempting to fulfill our national purpose; to create and sustain a society in which all of us are equal.

Throughout our history, when people have looked for new ways to solve their problems, and to uphold the principles of this nation, many times they have turned to political parties. They have often turned to the Democratic party.

What is it, what is it about the Democratic party that makes it the instrument that people use when they search for ways to shape their future? Well I believe the answer to that question lies in our concept of governing. Our concept of governing is derived from our view of people. It is a concept deeply rooted in a set of beliefs firmly etched in the national conscience, of all of us.

Now what are these beliefs?

First, we believe in equality for all and privileges for none. This is a belief that each American regardless of background has equal standing in the public forum, all of us. Because we believe this idea so firmly, we are an inclusive rather than an exclusive party. Let everybody come.

I think it no accident that most of those emigrating to

America in the nineteenth century identified with the Democratic party. We are a heterogeneous party made up of Americans of diverse backgrounds.

We believe that the people are the source of all governmental power; that the authority of the people is to be extended, not restricted. This can be accomplished only by providing each citizen with every opportunity to participate in the management of the government. They must have that.

We believe that the government which represents the authority of all the people, not just one interest group, but all the people, has an obligation to actively underscore, actively seek to remove those obstacles which would block individual achievement . . . obstacles emanating from race, sex, economic condition. The government must seek to remove them.

We are a party of innovation. We do not reject our traditions, but we are willing to adapt to changing circumstances, when change we must. We are willing to suffer the discomfort of change in order to achieve a better future.

We have a positive vision of the future founded on the belief that the gap between the promise and reality of America can one day be finally closed. We believe that.

This, my friends, is the bedrock of our concept of governing. This is a part of the reason why Americans have turned to the Democratic party. These are the foundations upon which a national community can be built.

Let's all understand that these guiding principles cannot be discarded for short-term political gains. They represent what this country is all about. They are indigenous to the American idea. And these are principles which are not negotiable.

In other times, I could stand here and give this kind of exposition on the beliefs of the Democratic party and that would be enough. But today that is not enough. People want more. That is not sufficient reason for the majority of the people of this country to vote Democratic. We have made mistakes. In our haste to do all things for all people, we did not foresee the full consequences of our actions. And when the people raised their voices, we didn't hear. But our deafness was only a temporary condition, and not an irreversible condition.

Even as I stand here and admit that we have made mistakes I still believe that as the people of America sit in judgment on each party, they will recognize that our mistakes were mistakes of the heart. They'll recognize that.

And now we must look to the future. Let us heed the voice of the people and recognize their common sense. If we do not, we not only blaspheme our political heritage, we ignore the common ties that bind all Americans.

Many fear the future. Many are distrustful of their leaders, and believe that their voices are never heard. Many seek only to satisfy their private work wants. To satisfy private interests.

But this is the great danger America faces. That we will cease to be one nation and become instead a collection of interest groups; city against suburb, region against region, individual against individual. Each seeking to satisfy private wants.

If that happens, who then will speak for America?

Who then will speak for the common good?

This is the question which must be answered in 1976.

Are we to be one people bound together by common spirit sharing in a common endeavor or will we become a divided nation?

For all of its uncertainty, we cannot flee the future. We must not become the new puritans and reject our society. We must address and master the future together. It can be done if we restore the belief that we share a sense of national community, that we share a common national endeavor. It can be done.

There is no executive order; there is no law that can require the American people to form a national community. This we must do as individuals and if we do it as individuals, there is no President of the United States who can veto that decision.

As a first step, we must restore our belief in ourselves. We are a generous people so why can't we be generous with each other? We need to take to heart the words spoken by Thomas Jefferson: "Let us restore to social intercourse that harmony and that affection without which liberty and even life are but dreary things."

A nation is formed by the willingness of each of us to share in the responsibility for upholding the common good.

A government is invigorated when each of us is willing to participate in shaping the future of this nation.

In this election year we must define the common good and begin again to shape a common good and begin again to shape a common future. Let each person do his or her part. If one citizen is unwilling to participate, all of us are going to suffer. For the American idea, though it is shared by all of us, is realized in each one of us.

And now, what are those of us who are elected public officials supposed to do? We call ourselves public servants but I'll tell you this: we as public servants must set an example for the rest of the nation. It is hypocritical for the public official to admonish and exhort the people to uphold the common good if we are derelict in upholding the common good. More is required of public officials than slogans and handshakes and press releases. More is required. We must hold ourselves strictly accountable. We must provide the people with a vision of the future.

If we promise as public officials, we must deliver. If we as public officials propose, we must produce. If we say to the American people it is time for you to be sacrificial; sacrifice. If the public official says that, we (public officials) must be the first to give. We must be. And again, if we make mistakes, we must be willing to admit them. We have to do that. What we have to do is strike a balance between the idea that government should do everything and the idea, the belief, that government ought to do nothing. Strike a balance.

Let there be no illusions about the difficulty of forming this kind of a national community. It's tough, difficult, not easy. But a spirit of harmony will survive in America only if each of us remembers that we share a common destiny. If each of us remembers when self-interest and bitterness seem to prevail, that we share a common destiny.

I have confidence that we can form this kind of national community.

I have confidence that the Democratic party can lead the way. I have that confidence. We cannot improve on the system of government handed down to us by the founders of the Republic, there is no way to improve upon that. But what we can do is to find new ways to implement that system and realize our destiny.

Now, I began this speech by commenting to you on the uniqueness of a Barbara Jordan making the keynote address. Well I am going to close my speech by quoting a Republican President and I ask you that as you listen to these words of Abraham Lincoln, relate them to the concept of a national community in which every last one of us participates: "As I would not be a slave, so I would not be a master."

This expresses my idea of Democracy. Whatever differs from this, to the extent of the difference is no democracy.

THE INAUGURAL ADDRESS [3]

JIMMY CARTER [4]

Unusual interest developed in President Jimmy Carter's first Inaugural Address because of the curiosity over how a southern peanut farmer, a "born again Christian," would approach his first official speech. Critics are wont to compare each inaugural with its predecessors.

What the public heard, of course, was not on a plane with the addresses of Woodrow Wilson, Franklin D. Roosevelt, or John F. Kennedy. William Safire, for instance, called it "a banal, forgettable speech" (New York *Times*, January 24, 1977), and *Time* thought it "notably subdued" (January 31, 1977). Richard L. Strout, on the other hand, conceded that it had "strength and dignity" (*Christian Science Monitor*, January 24, 1977), and, describing the whole Inaugural Day, including the speech, James Reston called it "a revival meeting right out of the old Chautauqua Circuit" (New York *Times*, January 21, 1977).

The following day a panel on "The Week In Review," a Public Broadcasting System program moderated by Paul Duke, demonstrated the mood of many reporters. One panelist declared Carter's inaugural "not a well written speech," another suggested it did "not read as well as it sounded," a third was amazed that Carter had actually written the speech himself, but he thought that "the verbs were weak." Agreeing that it did not measure up to what John F. Kennedy said in 1961, they nevertheless conceded that it was "filled with good will."

The new President spoke to about 150,000 on the frosty Capitol grounds. Concerning the preparation of the speech *Time* magazine reported:

> Carter had finished polishing his Inaugural Address only a couple of days earlier, working in longhand and with a typewriter at the large desk in the study of his ranch-style house in Plains. Speechwriter Patrick Anderson had written the first version, but Carter wrote at least three more drafts, sometimes spreading the paragraphs out like pieces of a jigsaw puzzle and Scotch-taping them into a new arrangement. In the final version, Anderson said, he recog-

[3] Delivered from a platform, built over the steps of the Capitol, Washington, D.C., January 20, 1977.

[4] For biographical note, see Appendix.

nized "only a few sentences here and there" of his own work.

After some reflection James Reston suggested that "Mr. Carter works by symbols" (New York *Times*, January 28, 1977). Probably herein was what many observers had missed. The essence of Carter's message was in the *man*. Whatever element of eloquence it possessed was to be found less in the words themselves than in the style of the speaker, as he read his short speech (only fourteen minutes and twenty-seven seconds long), as he graciously thanked retiring President Ford for his contribution, and a little later as the new President and his wife walked hand in hand down Pennsylvania Avenue, followed by their family.

The reader may wish to compare the Carter inaugural with his inaugural address as governor of Georgia on January 12, 1971 (REPRESENTATIVE AMERICAN SPEECHES: 1970-1971, p 142-6) and with President Nixon's address in 1973 (REPRESENTATIVE AMERICAN SPEECHES: 1972-73, p 15-21).

For myself and for our nation, I want to thank my predecessor for all he has done to heal our land.

In this outward and physical ceremony, we attest once again to the inner and spiritual strength of our nation. As my high school teacher, Miss Julia Coleman, used to say, "We must adjust to changing times and still hold to unchanging principles."

Here before me is the Bible used in the inauguration of our first President, in 1789, and I have just taken the oath of office on the Bible my mother gave me just a few years ago, opened to a timeless admonition from the ancient prophet Micah: "He hath showed thee, o man, what is good; and what doth the Lord require of thee, but to do justly, and to love mercy, and to walk humbly with thy God." (Micah 6:8)

This inauguration ceremony marks a new beginning, a new dedication within our government, and a new spirit among us all. A President may sense and proclaim that new spirit, but only a people can provide it.

Two centuries ago, our nation's birth was a milestone in the long quest for freedom. But the bold and brilliant dream which excited the Founders of this nation still awaits

its consummation. I have no new dream to set forth today, but rather urge a fresh faith in the old dream.

Ours was the first society openly to define itself in terms of both spirituality and human liberty. It is that unique self-definition which has given us an exceptional appeal— but it also imposes on us a special obligation to take on those moral duties which, when assumed, seem invariably to be in our own best interests.

You have given me a great responsibility—to stay close to you, to be worthy of you, and to exemplify what you are. Let us create together a new national spirit of unity and trust. Your strength can compensate for my weakness, and your wisdom can help to minimize my mistakes.

Let us learn together and laugh together and work together and pray together, confident that in the end we will triumph together in the right.

The American dream endures. We must once again have full faith in our country—and in one another. I believe America can be better. We can be even stronger than before.

Let our recent mistakes bring a resurgent commitment to the basic principles of our nation, for we know that if we despise our own government, we have no future. We recall special times when we have stood briefly, but magnificently, united. In those times no prize was beyond our grasp.

But we cannot dwell upon remembered glory. We cannot afford to drift. We reject the prospect of failure or mediocrity or an inferior quality of life for any person. Our government must at the same time be both competent and compassionate.

We have already found a high degree of personal liberty, and we are now struggling to enhance equality of opportunity. Our commitment to human rights must be absolute, our laws fair, our national beauty preserved; the powerful must not persecute the weak, and human dignity must be enhanced.

We have learned that *more* is not necessarily *better*, that even our great nation has its recognized limits, and that we can neither answer all questions nor solve all problems. We cannot afford to do everything, nor can we afford to lack boldness as we meet the future. So together, in a spirit of individual sacrifice for the common good, we must simply do our best.

Our nation can be strong abroad only if it is strong at home. And we know that the best way to enhance freedom in other lands is to demonstrate here that our democratic system is worthy of emulation.

To be true to ourselves, we must be true to others. We will not behave in foreign places so as to violate our rules and standards here at home, for we know that the trust which our nation earns is essential to our strength.

The world itself is now dominated by a new spirit. Peoples more numerous and more politically aware are craving, and now demanding, their place in the sun—not just for the benefit of their own physical condition, but for basic human rights.

The passion for freedom is on the rise. Tapping this new spirit, there can be no nobler nor more ambitious task for America to undertake on this day of a new beginning than to help shape a just and peaceful world that is truly humane.

We are a strong nation, and we will maintain strength so sufficient that it need not be proven in combat—a quiet strength based not merely on the size of an arsenal, but on the nobility of ideas.

We will be ever vigilant and never vulnerable, and we will fight our wars against poverty, ignorance, and injustice, for those are the enemies against which our forces can be honorably marshalled.

We are a proudly idealistic nation, but let no one confuse our idealism with weakness.

Because we are free, we can never be indifferent to the fate of freedom elsewhere. Our moral sense dictates a clear-cut preference for those societies which share with us an abiding respect for individual human rights. We do not seek to intimidate, but it is clear that a world which others can dominate with impunity would be inhospitable to decency and a threat to the well-being of all people.

The world is still engaged in a massive armaments race designed to ensure continuing equivalent strength among potential adversaries. We pledge perseverance and wisdom in our efforts to limit the world's armaments to those necessary for each nation's own domestic safety. And we will move this year a step toward our ultimate goal—the elimination of all nuclear weapons from this earth. We urge all other people to join us, for success can mean life instead of death.

Within us, the people of the United States, there is evident a serious and purposeful rekindling of confidence. And I join in the hope that when my time as your President has ended, people might say this about our nation:

—that we had remembered the words of Micah and renewed our search for humility, mercy, and justice;

—that we had torn down the barriers that separated those of different race and region and religion and where there had been mistrust, built unity, with a respect for diversity;

—that we had found productive work for those able to perform it;

—that we had strengthened the American family, which is the basis of our society;

—that we had ensured respect for the law and equal treatment under the law, for the weak and the powerful, for the rich and the poor; and

—that we had enabled our people to be proud of their own government once again.

I would hope that the nations of the world might say that we had built a lasting peace, based not on weapons of

war but on international policies which reflect our own
most precious values.

These are not just my goals—and they will not be my
accomplishments—but the affirmation of our nation's continuing moral strength and our belief in an undiminished,
ever-expanding American dream.

Thank you very much.

A BIBLICAL FAITH FOR A PRESIDENT [5]

Paul Moore Jr.[6]

On Sunday, November 21, 1976, at the 11:00 A.M. service in the vast Cathedral Church of St. John the Divine, the Rt. Rev. Paul Moore Jr., bishop of New York (Episcopal), directed his sermon toward setting forth what he considered the responsibilities that newly elected Jimmy Carter would soon face upon inauguration. On Sundays, large numbers of out-of-town visitors come to hear Bishop Moore, known for his efforts in the field of civil rights and his outspoken pronouncements on social issues facing the city and the nation.

The bishop, who is six feet five inches tall and makes an impressive appearance in his robes, entered at the west end of the cathedral. The procession moved slowly up the aisle to the high altar, and the liturgy began. The sermon that followed provided inspirational and hortative appeals to the new President as well as criteria for measuring his future course of action. Into the development the minister inserted specific references to the city's problems: "despair," "bread for children," "social justice for poor people," "gang warfare," and "juvenile crime."

The sermon is a plea for understanding, righteousness, compassion, and trust in God. It is a topical sermon with a social emphasis undergirded by numerous scriptural citations. In its theme, organization, development, and language it is an excellent example of homiletic appeal.

The next President of the United States stands in the biting wind of Inaugural Day. He is surrounded by crowds but stands alone. If he dares comprehend his vocation he must tremble so to do. Is this a Godly call to be fired with such ambition as to seek such power? What strange chemistry within a man's mind that propels him down two years of exhausting chase to seek an office too great for any man! I am sure Mr. Carter would describe this process as a vocation, a call: That is, an understanding of what you are

[5] Delivered at the Church of St. John the Divine, New York City, November 21, 1976. Quoted by permission.
[6] For biographical note, see Appendix.

24

meant to do; the fitting of the moral imperative to the individual person; and more—the sense that the ultimate mystery of being we call God somehow asks—somehow demands you—to take up the burden of a special task.

When our next President stands in that January wind he will have this sense of vocation—in this high office we can call it a sense of destiny.

As I read of the vast wilderness of responsibilities, the infinite number of decisions, the cacophony of special lobbies, the mounting Greek chorus of journalistic comment surrounding Mr. Carter, I hesitate to add even a whisper that may not reach his ears. And yet, amongst the pressures and persuasions from without we speak here today to encourage him to continue listening to the still small voice from within. We encourage him to stay his balance by putting himself in the presence of God's Peace. And we do presume to spell out what we believe a President is called upon to do who publicly has stated that he shares the Jewish and Christian understanding of reality found in the Bible.

Here are some thoughts on the implications of a clearly defined biblical faith for a President of the United States:

1. *He must be a man of compassion.* In Isaiah it is written "The Spirit of the Lord God is upon me; because the Lord hath anointed me to preach good tidings unto the meek; he hath sent me to bind up the brokenhearted, to proclaim liberty to the captives, and the opening of the prison to them that are bound." (Isaiah 61:1) Jesus said, "If you have done it unto one of the least of these my brethren you have done it unto me." His heart should have inscribed upon it the words on the Statue of Liberty: "Give me your tired, your poor, your huddled masses yearning to breathe free." Nor can he rest content until every soul in the United States can be housed, fed, and offered a job to do. This means beginning to close the gap between the rich and the poor, whatever the price may be. For if the gap grows wider the rich will live in increasing fear, and the poor in increasing desperation.

Compassion in the United States means, among other things, an understanding of the urban poor. I have urged Mr. Carter to visit the South Bronx; his office replied that he intended to do so. There, standing in the rubble of the failure of urban policy he can feel the despair of the urban poor and he must understand that only a vigorous urban federal policy can save them—in a sense, only he can save them.

Compassion lifts up the goal of security and freedom for all. The freedom of a democracy is measured by the freedom of its humblest citizen. A person cannot be politically or spiritually free if his very existence is twisted by generations of poverty. Thus *WELFARE* must be reformed so that those who receive it need not choose between their self-respect and bread for their children, so that the system will encourage them in seeking employment and in maintaining a stable home. Toward this end leaders in both parties suggest some form of income maintenance coupled with the availability of jobs provided, if need be, by the public sector or by public subsidy of the private sector.

Furthermore to fulfill biblical demands of social justice in a nation where poor people from all over the land and from foreign shores crowd into certain cities, the federal government must take responsibility for a uniform and a federally subsidized welfare system.

2. *He must be a catholic man, a universal man.* "Who is my neighbor?" they asked, and Jesus told the story of the good Samaritan—that any person in need is my neighbor. Because the President's influence stretches around the globe, so must his concern. Can a sane human being accept such a cross? Woodrow Wilson once did and was broken by it. Teddy Roosevelt had pretensions of being a sort of global godfather and has been ridiculed by history for paternalism toward those he called his little brown brothers. President Kennedy caught a vision and had a brief response to a global Camelot. I trust Mr. Carter is too tough to be a Wilson, too enlightened to be a Teddy Roosevelt, too conscious

of the tired frustrated 1970s to dare the Kennedy *hubris*. And yet he is the most powerful man in the world and when he speaks and when he moves he will have upon him the eyes, the suffering eyes, of the multitudes of the world. To them he must struggle to respond, and be seen to struggle to respond, whatever their ideology. Economic foreign aid is not a proper instrument of foreign policy. The best and most effective foreign policy is to be even handed to the poor of the world.

3. *He must be a man of peace.* Courage for peace far exceeds the courage for war. Mr. Carter must know the phrase from the Psalms, "A horse is a vain thing to save a man." The most clearly obvious place to start the road to peace is by a ruthless control of arms sales. President Ford boasts that we are at peace. Are we at peace when American bombs are dropped from American planes—albeit by one foreign warrior on another? Are we at peace when black fingers pull the triggers of American rifles upon their black brothers? Who is to blame for the murder when a bystander provides switch blades to two men engaged in a fist fight? The cynicism of our arms trade is so obscene that it blinds our moral judgment. May a biblical President have the grace to see this and the courage to stop it now! I was brought up in a conservative and a patriotic home. However the merchants of death, as the Krupp family then were called, were feared and hated there. The United States in 1976 makes the Krupp works of the 1920s look like a spitball factory.

But, as Mr. Carter knows, peace begins in the heart. The arms salesmen, the Pentagon and those who benefit by them use the time-tested propaganda of a strong America. Mr. Carter himself has used this phrase in reference to arms. But he also has begun to awaken within us our deeper understanding of strength—namely, an America of integrity and compassion and peace. A religious President has the obligation to change the concept of patriotism from a cheap, swaggering chauvinism to a real belief in the principles of the Declaration of Independence.

4. *He must be a man of extraordinary courage.* Americans admire courage more than any other virtue. From Elijah to Saint Peter the spiritual leaders of the Bible were persons of courage. No act of spiritual courage could so excite the admiration of our people as a full-blown assault on organized crime. Like the sale of arms the enormity of this situation so surrounds us that we accept it without realizing its incongruity. The mob is an accepted part of American life. The deaths of these leaders are reported like the death of any other prominent business leader. Descriptions of the gang warfare taking place on the city streets reads as calmly as the score of the football leagues. How come? How can we deal with juvenile crime with such subliminal training in the arbitrariness of the law? The CIA has successfully subverted foreign governments. Could its energies and the energies of the FBI be *really* turned to subvert organized crime, or must the President also tremble before its barons?

5. *He must be a truthful man.* "The truth will make you free." May he stand for open decisions. May he only be tempted by secrecy if the very life of our nation depends upon it. May he eschew corruption like the plague.

6. *Most important, as a Bible man he must believe that each man and woman is made in the image of God.* This belief leads not only to compassion for every child of God, but to an understanding of the divine spark in everyone which awaits the fanning of the wind of the Spirit. "Ask not what your country can do for you, but what you can do for your country." After eight years of a passive presidency in the midst of post-war affluence, after eight years of the doctrinaire cold war, President Kennedy said those words and a whole generation throughout the world responded because they wanted to believe. Look, Mr. President, there are millions ready to follow *you now.* Look, Mr. President, there are millions more who slumber but who can be called to sacrifice if they are asked by a leader in whose integrity they can believe. America wants to be proud of itself, not of its arms. America is willing to sacrifice, if the goal is a goal of

high humanity, if our leader is clearly motivated by the shining ethic of the book he knows so well.

We have forgotten, Mr. President, how great we can be. Hold up before us, by your word and action, the holy mirror of the Bible, so that we can see ourselves as we are made to be. After so long a sleep America is ready to be awakened. After so long a time of selfishness I believe America is now ready to sacrifice. Trust and follow your God and we will trust and follow you.

DEMOCRACY IN ACTION

THE THIRD PRESIDENTIAL DEBATE [1]

GERALD R. FORD — JIMMY CARTER [2]

One of the distinguishing features of the 1976 presidential campaign was the three debates between the presidential candidates Gerald Ford and Jimmy Carter and the single encounter between their running mates Robert J. Dole and Walter F. Mondale. Contrary to the billing, the so-called debates were "little more than joint press conferences and not very good press conferences at that" (Roscoe Drummond, *Christian Science Monitor*, October 27, 1976), or, as another source labeled them, "televised disputation" (David M. Alpern and others, *Newsweek*, September 27, 1976). Nevertheless the encounters served the useful function of letting the voters see the four principals answer tough questions from alert reporters.

Each debate was ninety minutes long. The first debate was held at the Walnut Street Theatre in Philadelphia, September 23, 1976; the second, at the Palace of Fine Arts Theatre, San Francisco, October 6, 1976; and the third in Phi Beta Kappa Memorial Hall at the College of William and Mary, Williamsburg, Virginia, October 22, 1976. Under the sponsorship of the League of Women Voters the debates were broadcast over the four networks, reaching perhaps as many as eighty-five to ninety-five million viewers.

Using a similar format the vice presidential candidates Mondale and Dole on October 15, 1976, met at Alley Theatre, Houston, Texas.

Included in this volume is a portion of the third presidential debate, considered by some to be the best of the three. Unlike the first two meetings in which the questions were limited to domestic issues (September 23) and foreign affairs (October 6), the third debate permitted inquiries on many issues. The panelists posed questions on subjects ranging from Watergate, the environment, and voter apathy to foreign affairs. Reproduced here are six of the fourteen subjects discussed. The introduction by

[1] Delivered on the evening of October 22, 1976, from Phi Beta Kappa Memorial Hall, College of William and Mary, Williamsburg, Virginia. Taken from *Weekly Compilation of Presidential Documents*, vol. 12, no. 44, p 1563-78.

[2] For biographical notes, see Appendix.

Barbara Walters outlines the format and the two closing statements present the overall philosophies of Ford and Carter.

The outcome of these confrontations was inconclusive. It was generally conceded that President Ford made a slightly better impression during the first one, although the polls indicated a draw. During the second Jimmy Carter was more aggressive and forceful. The third was generally pronounced a draw. One observer suggested:

> The final debate was probably more enlightening on issue positions than the earlier ones. The questions were more specific and the answers were more responsive.
>
> In the preceding two contests Ford and Carter often blurred their positions, and the distinctions between them, by a variety of obfuscatory devices—torrents of selectively chosen statistics, hyperbole borrowed from their stump speeches and, sometimes, what appeared to be downright dissembling (Robert Shogan of the Los Angeles *Times*, reprinted in *State Times*, Baton Rouge, Louisiana, October 23, 1976).

THE MODERATOR: Good evening, I am Barbara Walters, moderator of the last of the debates of 1976 between Gerald R. Ford, Republican candidate for President, and Jimmy Carter, Democratic candidate for President.

Welcome, President Ford, welcome, Governor Carter, and thank you for joining us this evening.

This debate takes place before an audience in Phi Beta Kappa Memorial Hall on the campus of the College of William and Mary in historic Williamsburg, Virginia. It is particularly appropriate in this Bicentennial Year that we meet on these grounds to hear this debate. Two hundred years ago, five William and Mary students met at nearby Raleigh Tavern to form Phi Beta Kappa, a fraternity designed, they wrote, "to search out and dispel the clouds of falsehood by debating without reserve the issues of the day."

In that spirit of debate—"without reserve," "to dispel the clouds of falsehood"—gentlemen, let us proceed.

The subject matter of this debate is open, covering all issues and topics. Our questioners tonight are Joseph

Kraft, syndicated columnist; Robert Maynard, editorial writer for the Washington *Post*; and Jack Nelson, Washington bureau chief of the Los Angeles *Times*.

The ground rules tonight are as follows: Questioners will alternate questions between the candidates. The candidate has up to two and one half minutes to answer the question. The other candidate then has up to two minutes to respond. If necessary, a questioner may ask a follow-up question for further clarification and, in that case, the candidate has up to two minutes to respond. As was initially agreed to by both candidates, the answers should be responsive to the particular questions. Finally, each candidate has up to three minutes for a closing statement.

President Ford and Governor Carter do not have prepared notes or comments with them this evening, but they may make notes and refer to them during the debate.

It has been determined that President Ford would take the first question in this last debate, and, Mr. Kraft, you have that first question for President Ford.

MR. KRAFT: Mr. President, I assume that the Americans all know that these are difficult times and that there is no pie in the sky and that they don't expect something for nothing. So I'd like to ask you, as a first question, as you look ahead in the next four years, what sacrifices are you going to call on the American people to make? What price are you going to ask them to pay to realize your objectives?

Let me add, Governor Carter, that if you felt that it was appropriate to answer that question in your comments, as to what price it would be appropriate for the American people to pay for a Carter Administration, I think that would be proper, too.

Mr. President?

THE PRESIDENT: Mr. Kraft, I believe that the American people in the next four years, under a Ford Administration, will be called upon to make those necessary sacrifices to preserve the peace—which we have—which means, of course, that we will have to maintain an adequate military capability; which means, of course, that we will have to add, I think, a few billion dollars to our defense appropriations to make certain that we have adequate strategic forces, adequate conventional forces.

I think the American people will be called upon to be in the forefront in giving leadership to the solution of those problems that must be solved in the Middle East, in southern Africa, and any problems that might arise in the Pacific.

The American people will be called upon to tighten their belts a bit in meeting some of the problems that we face domestically. I don't think that America can go on a big spending spree with a whole lot of new programs that would add significantly to the federal budget.

I believe that the American people, if given the leadership that I would expect to give, would be willing to give this thrust to preserve the peace and the necessary restraint at home to hold the lid on spending so that we could, I think, have a long overdue and totally justified tax decrease for the middle-income people. And then—with the economy that would be generated from a restraint on spending and a tax reduction primarily for the middle-income people—then I think the American people would be willing to make those sacrifices for peace and prosperity in the next four years.

MR. KRAFT: Could I be a little more specific, Mr. President?

THE PRESIDENT: Sure, sure.

MR. KRAFT: Doesn't your policy really imply that we are going to have to have a pretty high rate of unemployment over a fairly long time, that growth is going to be fairly slow, and that we are not going to be able to do very much in the next four or five years to meet the basic agenda of our national needs in the cities, in health, in transit, and a whole lot of other things like that?

THE PRESIDENT: Not at all.

MR. KRAFT: Aren't those the real costs?

THE PRESIDENT: No, Mr. Kraft. We're spending very significant amounts of money now, some $200 billion a year, almost 50 percent of our total federal expenditure by the federal government at the present time, for human needs. Now we will probably have to increase that to some extent, but we don't have to have growth in spending that will blow the lid off and add to the problems of inflation.

I believe we can meet the problems within the cities of this country and still give a tax reduction. I proposed, as you know, a reduction to increase the personal exemption from $750 to $1,000, with the fiscal program that I have. And if you look at the projections, it shows that we will reduce unemployment, that we will continue to win the battle against inflation and, at the same time, give the kind of quality of life that I believe is possible in America: a job, a home for all those that will work and save for it, safety in the streets, health care that is affordable. These things can be done if we have the right vision and the right restraint and the right leadership.

THE MODERATOR: Thank you. Governor Carter, your response, please.

MR. CARTER: Well, I might say first of all, that I think in case of a Carter Administration, the sacrifices would be much less. Mr. Ford's own environmental agency has projected a 10 percent unemployment rate by 1978 if he is President. The American people are ready to make sacrifices if they are part of the process, if they know that they will be helping to make decisions and won't be excluded from being an involved party to the national purpose.

The major effort that we must put forward is to put our people back to work. And I think that this is one example where a lot of people have selfish, grasping ideas now. I remember in 1973, in the depth of the energy crisis, when President Nixon called on the American people to make a sacrifice to cut down on the waste of gasoline, to cut down on the speed of automobiles. It was a tremendous surge of patriotism. "I want to make a sacrifice for my country."

I think we could call together—with strong leadership

in the White House—business, industry, and labor, and say, let's have voluntary price restraints, let's lay down some guidelines so we don't have continuing inflation.

We could also have an end to the extremes. We now have one extreme, for instance, of some welfare recipients who by taking advantage of the welfare laws, the housing laws, the Medicaid laws, and the food stamp laws, make over $10,000 a year, and they don't have to pay any taxes on it. At the other extreme, just 1 percent of the richest people in our country derive 25 percent of all the tax benefits. So both those extremes grasp for advantage, and the person who has to pay that expense is the middle-income family who is still working for a living. And they have to pay for the rich who have the privilege and for the poor who are not working.

But I think that a balanced approach, with everybody being part of it, and striving for unselfishness could help, as it did in 1973, to let people sacrifice for their own country. I know I'm ready for it; I think the American people are, too.

THE MODERATOR: Thank you. Mr. Maynard, your question to Governor Carter.

MR. MAYNARD: Governor, by all indications, the voters are so turned off by this election campaign so far that only half intend to vote. One major reason for this apathetic electorate appears to be the low level at which this campaign has been conducted. It has digressed frequently from important issues into allegations of blunders and brainwashing and fixations on lust in *Playboy*. What responsibility do you accept for the low level of this campaign for the nation's highest office?

MR. CARTER: I think the major reason for a decrease in participation that we've experienced ever since 1960 has been the deep discouragement of the American people about the performance of public officials. When you've got seven and one half to eight million people out of work, when you've got three times as much inflation as you had during the last eight-year Democratic Administration, when you have the highest deficits in history, when you have it becoming increasingly difficult for a family to put a child through college or to own a home, there is a natural inclination to be turned off. Also, in the aftermath of Vietnam and Cambodia and Watergate and the CIA revelations, people have felt that they've been betrayed by public officials.

I have to admit that in the heat of the campaign—I've been in thirty primaries during the springtime; I've been campaigning for twenty-two months—I've made some mistakes. And I think this is part of just being a human being. I have to say that my campaign has been an open one. The *Playboy* thing has been of very great concern to me. I don't know how to deal with it exactly. I agreed to give the interview to *Playboy*. Other people have done it who are notable—Governor Jerry Brown, Walter Cronkite, Albert Schweitzer, Mr. Ford's own Secretary of Treasury, Mr. Simon, William Buckley, many other people. But they weren't running for President. And in retrospect, from hindsight, I would not have given that interview had I to do it over again. If I should ever decide in the future to discuss my deep Christian beliefs and condemnation and sinfulness, I would use another forum besides *Playboy*.

But I can say this: I'm doing the best I can to get away from that. And during the next ten days, the American people will not see the Carter campaign running television advertisements or newspaper advertisements based on a personal attack on President Ford's character. I believe that the opposite is true with President Ford's campaign. And I hope that we can leave those issues, in the next ten days, about personalities and mistakes of the past—we've both made some mistakes—and talk about unemployment, inflation, housing, education, taxation, government organization, stripping away of secrecy, and the things that are crucial to the American people.

I regret the things in my own long campaign that have

been mistaken, but I'm trying to do away with those the last ten days.

THE MODERATOR: Thank you, Governor Carter. President Ford, your response?

THE PRESIDENT: I believe that the American people have been turned off in this election, Mr. Maynard, for a variety of reasons. We have seen on Capitol Hill, in the Congress, a great many allegations of wrongdoing, of alleged immorality. Those are very disturbing to the American people. They wonder how an elected representative can serve them and participate in such activities, serving in the Congress of the United States. Yes, and I'm certain many, many Americans were turned off by the revelations of Watergate, a very, very bad period of time in American political history. Yes, and thousands, maybe millions of Americans were turned off because of the problems that came out of our involvement in Vietnam.

But on the other hand, I found on July 4 of this year, a new spirit born in America. We were celebrating our Bicentennial. And I find that there is a movement—as I traveled around the country—of greater interest in this campaign. Now, like any hard-working person seeking public office, in the campaign, inevitably, sometimes you will use rather graphic language. And I am guilty of that just like, I think, most others in the political arena. But I do make a pledge, that in the next ten days when we are asking the American people to make one of the most important decisions in their lifetime, because I think this election is one of the most vital in the history of America, that we do together what we can to stimulate voter participation. . . .

THE MODERATOR: Mr. Nelson, your question now to Governor Carter.

MR. NELSON: Governor, despite the fact that you've been running for President a long time now, many Americans still seem to be uneasy about you. They don't feel that they know you or the people around you. And one problem seems to be that you haven't reached out to bring people with broad background or national experience into your campaign or your presidential plans. Most of the people around you on a day-to-day basis are the people you've known in Georgia. Many of them are young and relatively inexperienced in national affairs. Doesn't this raise a serious question as to whether you would bring into a Carter Administration people with the necessary background to run the federal government?

MR. CARTER: I don't believe it does. I began campaigning twenty-two months ago. At that time, nobody thought I had a chance to win. Very few people knew who I was. I came from a tiny town, as you know—Plains—and didn't hold public office, didn't have very much money. And my first organization was just four or five people plus my wife and my children, my three sons and their wives.

And we won the nomination by going out into the streets, barbershops, beauty parlors, restaurants, stores, in factory-shift lines, also in farmers' markets and livestock-sale barns, and we talked a lot and we listened a lot, and we learned from the American people. We built up an awareness among the voters of this country, particularly those in whose primaries I entered—thirty of them, nobody has ever done that before—about who I was and what I stood for.

Now we have a very wide-ranging group of advisers who help me prepare for these debates and who teach me about international economics and foreign affairs, defense matters, health, education, welfare, government reorganization—I'd say several hundred of them, and they are very fine and very highly qualified.

The one major decision that I have made since acquiring the nomination—and I share this with President Ford —is the choice of the Vice President. I think this would be indicative of the kind of leaders that I would choose to help me if I am elected.

I chose Senator Walter Mondale. And the only criterion that I have put forward in my own mind was, who among the several million people in this country would be the best person qualified to be President if something should happen to me and to join me in being Vice President if I should serve out my term? And I'm convinced now, more than I was when I got the nomination, that Walter Mondale was the right choice. And I believe this is a good indication of the kind of people that I would choose in the future.

Mr. Ford has had that same choice to make. I don't want to say anything critical of Senator Dole, but I have never heard Mr. Ford say that that was his primary consideration—who is the best person I could choose in this country to be President of the United States.

I feel completely at ease knowing that some day Senator Mondale might very well be President. In the last five vice presidential nominees, incumbents, three of them have become President. But I think this is indicative of what I would do.

THE MODERATOR: President Ford, your response please.

THE PRESIDENT: The governor may not have heard my established criteria for the selection of a Vice President, but it was a well-established criteria that the person I selected would be fully qualified to be President of the United States. And Senator Bob Dole is so qualified—sixteen years in the House of Representatives and in the Senate, very high responsibilities on important committees.

I don't mean to be critical of Senator Mondale, but I was very, very surprised when I read that Senator Mondale made a very derogatory, very personal comment about General Brown after the news story that broke about General Brown. If my recollection is correct, he indicated that General Brown was not qualified to be a sewer commissioner. I don't think that's a proper way to describe a chairman of the Joint Chiefs of Staff who has fought for his country for thirty-five years. And I'm sure the governor would agree with me on that.

I think Senator Dole would show more good judgment

and discretion than to so describe a heroic and brave and very outstanding leader of the military.

So I think our selection of Bob Dole as Vice President is based on merit. And if he should ever become the President of the United States, with his vast experience as a member of the House and a member of the Senate, as well as a Vice President, I think he would do an outstanding job as President of the United States. . . .

THE MODERATOR: Mr. Maynard, to President Ford.

MR. MAYNARD: Mr. President, twice you have been the intended victim of would-be assassins using handguns, yet you remain a steadfast opponent of substantive handgun control. There are now some 40 million handguns in this country, going up at the rate of 2.5 million a year, and tragically those handguns are frequently purchased for self-protection and wind up being used against a relative or a friend. In light of that, why do you remain so adamant in your opposition to substantive gun control in this country?

THE PRESIDENT: Mr. Maynard, the record of gun control, whether it's in one city or another or in some states does not show that the registration of a gun, handgun, or the registration of the gun owner has in any way whatsoever decreased the crime rate or the use of that gun in the committing of a crime. The record just doesn't prove that such legislation or action by a local city council is effective.

What we have to do—and this is the crux of the matter—is to make it very, very difficult for a person who uses a gun in the commission of a crime to stay out of jail. If we make the use of a gun in the commission of a crime a serious criminal offense and that person is prosecuted, then in my opinion we are going after the person who uses the gun for the wrong reason. I don't believe in the registration of handguns or the registration of the handgun owner. That has not proven to be effective. And, therefore, I think the better way is to go after the criminal, the individual who commits a crime in the possession of a gun and uses that gun for a part of his criminal activity.

Those are the people who ought to be in jail. And the only way to do it is to pass strong legislation so that once apprehended, indicted, convicted, they will be in jail and off the streets and not using guns in the commission of a crime.

MR. MAYNARD: But, Mr. President, don't you think that the proliferation of the availability of handguns contributes to the possibility of those crimes being committed? And there is a second part to my follow-up. Very quickly, there are, as you know and as you've said, jurisdictions around the country with strong gun control laws. The police officials in those cities contend that if there were a national law to prevent other jurisdictions from providing the weapons that then come into places like New York, that they might have a better handle on the problem. Have you considered that in your analysis of the handgun proliferation problem?

THE PRESIDENT: Yes, I have, and the individuals with whom I have consulted have not convinced me that a national registration of handguns or handgun owners will solve the problem you are talking about. The person who wants to use a gun for an illegal purpose can get it whether it's registered or outlawed—they will be obtained—and they are the people who ought to go behind bars. You should not, in the process, penalize the legitimate handgun owner. And when you go through the process of registration, you, in effect, are penalizing that individual who uses his gun for a very legitimate purpose.

THE MODERATOR: Governor Carter.

MR. CARTER: I think it's accurate to say that Mr. Ford's position on gun control has changed. Earlier, Mr. Levi, his Attorney General, put forward a gun control proposal which Mr. Ford later, I believe, espoused that called for the prohibition against the sale of the so-called "Saturday night specials." It would have put very strict control over who owned a handgun.

I have been a hunter all my life and happen to own both shotguns, rifles, and a handgun. And the only purpose that I would see in registering handguns and not long guns of any kind would be to prohibit the ownership of those guns by those who have used them in the commission of a crime or who have been proven to be mentally incompetent to own a gun. I believe that limited approach to the question would be advisable, and I think adequate, but that's as far as I would go with it. . . .

THE MODERATOR: Mr. Kraft.

MR. KRAFT: Mr. President, the country is now in something that your advisers call an economic pause. I think to most Americans that sounds like an antiseptic term for low growth, unemployment, standstill at a high, high level, decline in take-home pay, lower factory earnings, more layoffs. Isn't that really a rotten record, and doesn't your Administration bear most of the blame for it?

THE PRESIDENT: Well, Mr. Kraft, I violently disagree with your assessment, and I don't think the record justifies the conclusion that you come to. Let me talk about the economic announcements that were made just this past week.

Yes, it was announced that the GNP real growth in the third quarter was at 4 percent. But, do you realize that over the last ten years that's a higher figure than the average growth during the ten-year period. Now, it's lower than the 9.2 percent growth in the first quarter and it's lower than the 5 percent growth in the second quarter. But, every economist—liberal, conservative—that I am familiar with, recognizes that in the fourth quarter of this year and in the first quarter of next year that we will have an increase in real GNP.

But now let's talk about the pluses that came out this week. We had an 18 percent increase in housing starts. We had a substantial increase in new permits for housing. As a matter of fact, based on the announcement this week, there will be at an annual rate, 1 million 800-some thousand new houses built, which is a tremendous increase over last year and a substantial increase over the earlier part of this year.

Now, in addition, we had some very good news in the reduction in the rate of inflation, and inflation hits everybody—those who are working and those who are on welfare. The rate of inflation, as announced just the other day, is under 5 percent, and the 4.4 percent that was indicated at the time of the 4 percent GNP, was less than the 5.4 percent. It means that the American buyer is getting a better bargain today because inflation is less.

MR. KRAFT: Mr. President, let me ask you this: There has been an increase in layoffs, and that's something that bothers everybody because even people that have a job are afraid they are going to be fired. Did you predict that increase in layoffs? Didn't that take you by surprise? Hasn't your Administration been surprised by this pause? In fact, haven't you been so obsessed with saving money that you didn't even push the government to spend funds that were allocated?

THE PRESIDENT: Mr. Kraft, I think the record can be put in this way, which is the way that I think satisfies most Americans: Since the depths of the recession, we have added 4 million jobs. Most importantly, consumer confidence, as surveyed by the reputable organization at the University of Michigan, is at the highest since 1972.

In other words, there is a growing public confidence in the strength of this economy. And that means that there will be more industrial activity; it means that there will be a reduction in the unemployment; it means that there will be increased hires; it means that there will be increased employment.

Now, we've had this pause but most economists, regardless of their political philosophy, indicate that this pause for a month or two was healthy because we could not have honestly sustained a 9.2 percent rate of growth, which we had in the first quarter of this year.

Now, I'd like to point out as well that the United States economic recovery from the recession of a year ago is well ahead of the economic recovery of any major free industrial nation in the world today. We are ahead of all of the Western European countries. We are ahead of Japan. The United States is leading the free world out of the recession that was serious a year and a half ago.

We are going to see unemployment going down, more jobs available, and the rate of inflation going down. And I think this is a record that the American people understand and will appreciate.

THE MODERATOR: Governor Carter.

MR. CARTER: Well, with all due respect to President Ford, I think he ought to be ashamed of making that statement because we have the highest unemployment rate now that we had at any time between the Great Depression, caused by Herbert Hoover, and the time President Ford took office. We have got seven and one half million people out of jobs. Since he has been in office, two and one half million more American people have lost their jobs. In the last four months alone, 500,000 Americans have gone on the unemployment rolls. In the last month, we've had a net loss of 163,000 jobs.

Anybody who says that the inflation rate is in good shape now ought to talk to the housewives. One of the overwhelming results that I have seen in places is people feel that you can't plan any more, there is no way to make a prediction that my family might be able to own a home or to put my kids through college. Savings accounts are losing money instead of gaining money. Inflation is robbing us.

Under the present administrations—Nixon's and Ford's —we have had three times the inflation rate that we experienced under President Johnson and President Kennedy. The economic growth is less than half today what it was at the beginning of this year. And housing starts—he compares the housing starts with last year, I don't blame him because in 1975 we had fewer housing starts in this country, fewer homes built than any year since 1940. That's thirty-five years. And we've got a thirty-five percent unemployment rate in many areas of this country among construction workers. And Mr. Ford hasn't done anything about it. And I think this shows a callous indifference to the families that have suffered so much. He has vetoed bills passed by Congress within the congressional budget guidelines—job opportunities for 2 million Americans. We will never have a balanced budget, we will never meet the needs of our people, we will never control the inflationary spiral as long as we have seven and one half or eight million people out of work who are looking for jobs. And we have probably got two and one half more million people who are not looking for jobs any more because they've given up hope. That is a very serious indictment of this Administration. It's probably the worst one of all.

THE MODERATOR: Mr. Maynard.

MR. MAYNARD: Governor Carter, you entered this race against President Ford with a twenty-point lead or better in the polls and now it appears that this campaign is headed for a photo finish. You have said how difficult it is to run against a sitting President but Mr. Ford was just as much an incumbent in July when you were twenty points ahead as he is now. Can you tell us what caused the evaporation of that lead, in your opinion?

MR. CARTER: Well, that's not exactly an accurate description of what happened. When I was that far ahead it was immediately following the Democratic convention and before the Republican convention. At that time 25 or 30 percent of the Reagan supporters said that they would not support President Ford, but as occurred at the end of the Democratic Convention, the Republican party unified itself, and I think immediately following the Republican convention there was about a ten point spread. I believe that to be accurate. I had 49 percent; President Ford had 39 percent.

The polls are good indications of fluctuations, but they vary widely one from another, and the only poll I've ever followed is the one that, you know, is taken on Election Day. I was in thirty primaries in the spring and at first it was obvious that I didn't have any standing in the polls.

As a matter of fact, I think when Gallup ran their first poll in December 1975 they didn't even put my name on the list. They had thirty-five people on the list—my name wasn't even there. At the beginning of the year, I had about 2 percent. So the polls, to me, are interesting, but they don't determine my hopes or my despair.

I campaign among people. I have never depended on powerful political figures to put me in office. I have a direct relationship with hundreds of thousands of people around the country who actively campaign for me. In Georgia alone, for instance, I got 84 percent of the vote, and I think there were fourteen people in addition to myself on the ballot, and Governor Wallace had been very strong in Georgia. That is an overwhelming support from my own people who know me best. And today we have about five hundred Georgians at their own expense, just working people who believe in me, spread around the country involved in the political campaign.

So the polls are interesting, but I don't know how to explain the fluctuations. I think a lot of it depends on current events—sometimes foreign affairs, sometimes domestic affairs. But I think our core of support among those who are crucial to the election has been fairly steady. And my success in the primary season was, I think, notable for a newcomer, from someone who's outside of Washington who never has been a part of the Washington establishment. And I think that we will have a good result on November 2 for myself and I hope for the country.

THE MODERATOR: President Ford, your response.

THE PRESIDENT: I think the increase in the prospects as far as I am concerned and the less favorable prospects for Governor Carter reflect that Governor Carter is inconsistent in many of the positions that he takes. He tends to distort on a number of occasions. Just a moment ago, for example, he was indicating that in the 1950s, for example, unemployment was very low. He fails to point out that in the 1950s we were engaged in the war in Vietnam—I mean in Korea.

We had 3.5 million young men in the Army, Navy, Air Force, and Marines. That's not the way to end unemployment or to reduce unemployment.

At the present time, we are at peace. We have reduced the number of people in the Army, Navy, Air Force, and Marines from 3.5 million to 2.1 million. We are not at war. We have reduced the military manpower by 1.4 million. If we had that many more people in the Army, the Navy, the Air Force, and Marines, our unemployment figure would be considerably less.

But this Administration doesn't believe the way to reduce unemployment is to go to war or to increase the number of people in the military. So, you cannot compare unemployment, as you sought to, at the present time, with the 1950s, because the then Administration had people in the military. They were at war. They were fighting overseas. And this Administration has reduced the size of the military by 1.4 million. They are in the civilian labor market, and they are not fighting anywhere around the world today.

THE MODERATOR: Thank you, gentlemen.

This will complete our questioning for this debate. We don't have time for more questions and full answers. So, now each candidate will be allowed up to four minutes for a closing statement. And, at the original coin toss in Philadelphia a month ago, it was determined that President Ford would make the first closing statement tonight.

President Ford.

THE PRESIDENT: For twenty-five years, I served in the Congress under five Presidents. I saw them work, I saw them make very hard decisions. I didn't always agree with their decisions, whether they were Democratic or Republican Presidents. For the last two years, I've been the President, and I have found from experience that it's much more difficult to make those decisions than it is to second guess them.

I became President at the time that the United States was in a very troubled time. We had inflation of over 12 percent; we were on the brink of the worst recession in the last forty years; we were still deeply involved in the problems of Vietnam; the American people had lost faith and trust and confidence in the presidency itself. That situation called for me to first put the United States on a steady course and to keep our keel well-balanced because we had to face the difficult problems that had all of a sudden hit America.

I think most people know that I did not seek the presidency, but I am asking for your help and assistance to be President for the next four years. During this campaign, we've seen a lot of television shows, a lot of bumper stickers, and a great many slogans of one kind or another, but those are not the things that count. What counts is that the United States celebrated its two hundredth birthday on July 4. As a result of that wonderful experience all over the United States, there is a new spirit in America. The American people are healed, are working together. The American people are moving again and moving in the right direction.

We have cut inflation by better than half. We have come out of the recession, and we are well on the road to real prosperity in this country again. There has been a restoration of faith and confidence and trust in the presidency because I've been open, candid, and forthright. I have never promised more than I could produce and I have produced everything that I promised. We are at peace—not a single young American is fighting or dying on any foreign soil tonight. We have peace with freedom.

I've been proud to be President of the United States during these very troubled times. I love America just as all of you love America. It would be the highest honor for me to have your support on November 2 and for you to say, "Jerry Ford, you've done a good job; keep on doing it."

Thank you and good night.

THE MODERATOR: Thank you, President Ford.

Governor Carter.

MR. CARTER: The major purpose of an election for President is to choose a leader, someone who can analyze the depths of feeling in our country, to set a standard for our people to follow, to inspire people to reach for greatness, to correct our defects, to answer difficulties, to bind ourselves together in a spirit of unity.

I don't believe the present Administration has done that. We have been discouraged and we've been alienated, sometimes we've been embarrassed, sometimes we've been ashamed. Our people are out of work, and there is a sense of withdrawal.

But our country is innately very strong. Mr. Ford is a good and decent man, but he has been in office now more than eight hundred days, approaching almost as long as John Kennedy was in office. I would like to ask the American people what has been accomplished. A lot remains to be done.

My own background is different from his. I was a school board member and a library board member, I served on a hospital authority, and I was in the state senate, and I was governor and I am an engineer, a naval officer, a farmer, a businessman. I believe we require someone who can work harmoniously with the Congress and can work closely with the people of this country, and who can bring a new image and a new spirit to Washington.

Our tax structure is a disgrace and needs to be reformed. I was governor of Georgia for four years. We never increased sales taxes or income tax or property taxes. As a matter of fact, the year before we went out of office we gave a $50 million refund to the property taxpayers of Georgia.

We spend $600 per person in this country, every man, woman, and child, for health care. We still rank fifteenth among all of the nations in the world in infant mortality, and our cancer rate is higher than any country in the world. We don't have good health care. We could have it.

Employment ought to be restored to our people. We have become almost a welfare state. We spend now 700 percent more on unemployment compensation than we did eight years ago when the Republicans took over the White House. Our people want to go back to work. Our education system can be improved. Secrecy ought to be stripped away from government, and a maximum of personal privacy ought to be maintained. Our housing programs have gone bad. It used to be that the average family could own a house, but now less than a third of our people can afford to buy their own homes.

The budget was more grossly out of balance last year than ever before in the history of our country—$65 billion —primarily because our people are not at work. Inflation is robbing us, as we've already discussed, and the government bureaucracy is just a horrible mess.

This doesn't have to be. I don't know all of the answers. Nobody could. But I do know that if the President of the United States and the Congress of the United States and the people of the United States said, "I believe our nation is greater than what we are now," I believe that if we are inspired, if we can achieve a degree of unity, if we can set our goals high enough and work toward recognized goals with industry and labor and agriculture along with government at all levels, we can achieve great things.

We might have to do it slowly. There are no magic answers to it, but I believe together we can make great progress, we can correct our difficult mistakes and answer those very tough questions.

I believe in the greatness of our country, and I believe the American people are ready for a change in Washington. We have been drifting too long. We have been dormant too long. We have been discouraged too long. And we have not set an example for our own people, but I believe that we can now establish in the White House a good relationship with Congress, a good relationship with our people, set very high goals for our country, and with inspiration and hard work we can achieve great things and let the world know—that's very important, but more importantly, let the people in our own country realize—that we still live in the greatest nation on earth.

Thank you very much.

THE MODERATOR: Thank you, Governor Carter, and thank you, President Ford. I also would like to thank the audience and my three colleagues—Mr. Kraft, Mr. Maynard, and Mr. Nelson, who have been our questioners.

This debate has, of course, been seen by millions of Americans, and in addition tonight is being broadcast to 113 nations throughout the world.

This concludes the 1976 presidential debates, a truly remarkable exercise in democracy for this is the first time in sixteen years that the presidential candidates have debated. It is the first time ever that an incumbent President has debated his challenger, and the debate included the first between the two vice presidential candidates.

President Ford and Governor Carter, we not only want to thank you but we commend you for agreeing to come together to discuss the issues before the American people.

And our special thanks to the League of Women Voters for making these events possible. In sponsoring these events, the League of Women Voters Education Fund has tried to provide you with the information that you will need to choose wisely.

The election is now only eleven days off. The candidates have participated in presenting their views in three, ninety-minute debates, and now it's up to the voters and now it is up to you to participate. The League urges all registered voters to vote on November 2 for the candidate of your choice.

And now, from Phi Beta Kappa Memorial Hall on the campus of the College of William and Mary, this is Barbara Walters wishing you all a good evening.

BROADCAST JOURNALISM:
SERVING THE DEMOCRATIC PROCESS [3]

JULIAN GOODMAN [4]

The staging of the presidential debates in 1976 raised issues perhaps more important and significant than anything that Gerald Ford or Jimmy Carter said or did. At issue was the responsibilities of the mass media to voters in a presidential election. Some other related questions are: Does the First Amendment to the Constitution guarantee to broadcast journalists complete freedom in handling events of the magnitude of the presidential debates? Do the present attempts to regulate the broadcasters result in poor news coverage? Should broadcast journalists have the same First Amendment rights as print journalists? Do viewers need to see and hear minor or third-party candidates as well as the two principal contenders? Should producers of television coverage be restricted in how they present political debates?

At the present time broadcasters must meet the requirement of Section 315 of the Federal Communications Act of 1934 which reads as follows:

> If any licensee shall permit any person who is a legally qualified candidate for any public office to use a broadcasting station, he shall afford equal opportunities to all other such candidates for that office in the use of such broadcasting station. . . . Provided, that such licensee shall have no power of censorship over the material broadcast under the provisions of this section. No obligation is hereby imposed upon any licensee to allow the use of its station by any such candidate.

The so-called equal-time provision requires that if a broadcaster makes time available to one candidate, he must provide equal opportunity to any other legally qualified opponent who requests it; hence, if a station affiliated with a network provides time to a Republican candidate, it must give equal opportunity to minor as well as other major candidates.

In 1960 the Kennedy-Nixon presidential debates were pos-

---

[3] Delivered to an all-college convocation at Walter Ford Hall, Ithaca College, Ithaca, New York, October 22, 1976. Quoted by permission.
[4] For biographical note, see Appendix.

sible because of a congressional suspension of the equal-time rule. In 1976 a new interpretation of the Federal Communications Commission opened the door for the Ford-Carter debates. "The ruling broadened the interpretation of 'bona fide news events,' which were not subject to the equal-time provision, by excluding from coverage under Section 315 all events that were sponsored by organizations independent of the broadcasting media." (See "How the Debates Came to Be," by Charles Benson, in *Britannica Book of the Year 1977*, p 701. The article is most informative as to how the debates were arranged.) Under the guidance of the League of Women Voters and with their financial support and much hard work on their part, the debates were carried as "bona fide news events." Although they cooperated, network officials were not enthusiastic about the arrangements. They were particularly vexed by the insistence of the League that cameras be focused upon the speakers with no shots of audience reaction. The reasoning behind the insistence was that selective shots of viewers could amount to editorializing.

Julian Goodman, chairman of the board of NBC, gives a persuasive presentation of the networks' points of view. The speech was made October 22, 1976, at a college convocation of about 250 students and faculty at Ithaca College, Ithaca, New York. It provides an overview of the context of the debates. Goodman forcefully states his position, saying "What is at stake is not camera shots or studio lighting. It is a principle. The principle that a journalist must be free to do his job. . . . You can't have a news medium that operates half free and half controlled."

I understand that many of you here are looking forward to careers in broadcast journalism.

I have spent more than thirty years in that profession, and I can tell you that it has its rewards and its exciting moments.

One of the highlights for me was sixteen years ago. I was vice president of NBC News then, and I had the responsibility for producing one of the four televised debates between John Kennedy and Richard Nixon. That was the first election in which we had such a confrontation between the presidential candidates of the two major parties before a nationwide television audience.

I have a vivid memory of going by the rooms where the candidates were waiting before the broadcast—in separated areas of the building—and finding each one standing in a quiet corner by himself, in what seemed to be an attitude of prayer.

I felt like a little praying myself. It was not only a tough test for the candidates. It was a test for NBC and for television. The medium had a chance to make an unprecedented contribution to the American electoral process. And it did.

The 1960 televised debates drew an audience of about 135 million people, and the turnout on Election Day set a record that hasn't been equaled since.

It is generally agreed that 1960 was a highwater mark for television's effectiveness in helping the nation choose its political leadership. It is no wonder that in the three national elections since 1960, broadcasters have sought the opportunity to broadcast presidential debates again. We've urged this before the Congress, the Federal Communications Commission and in other public forums, without success.

This year that did indeed come about. We have face-to-face debates between the presidential and vice presidential candidates, and the network news organizations have once again brought them to the people—and to tonight's conclusion.

It should follow that the public, as well as the network news managements, would be delighted and grateful. But neither seems as enthusiastic as might have been expected. In fact, before the Ford-Carter debates could go forward at all, there were difficult negotiations in which the networks raised a series of objections. At one point the arguing became so heated that the head of one network news organization left the meeting and suggested his network might not carry the debates.

There has been a good reason for these reservations but, unfortunately, the reasons may not be thoroughly understood. I'd like to talk a little about that today.

There is a basic difference between the current televised

debates and those of 1960. That difference is in the legal and regulatory framework that made the debates possible.

To put campaign debates on the air, the broadcaster has to overcome a tough obstacle, namely a provision of Section 315 of the Communications Act—the so-called equal-time rule.

The rule says that if a broadcaster makes time available to one candidate during an election campaign, he has to provide equal opportunity to any legally qualified opponent. And here the equal-time rule has a discouraging effect, because if the broadcaster offers free time for the appearance of major-party candidates, he is legally accessible to a flood of requests from minority-party candidates, most of whom have very little popular support, and even less prospect of being elected.

To make way for the 1960 debates, Congress suspended Section 315 for presidential and vice presidential candidates. This year Congress has not suspended the equal-time provision. The fact that it remains in effect makes the significant difference.

The debates this year are being held under a new FCC interpretation of Section 315. That interpretation says that presidential and vice presidential debates are exempt from equal-time requirements if they are held in the context of a news event. The FCC has said that to qualify, these events must take place under the auspices of somebody who is not a broadcaster. The nonbroadcaster who is filling that role in this campaign is the League of Women Voters.

And that's the basis for the networks' reservations.

It is not—as some have speculated—a question of whether cameras could cut away from the speakers to the audience, over who was to choose the reporters to ask the questions, over having pool coverage instead of each of the three networks providing unilateral coverage. It is not a question of the networks wanting to have their own way.

Let me make it clear that NBC—and I believe the other networks—are happy to cooperate with the League of

Women Voters. The League has performed a distinct public service in stepping forward to provide a needed national forum. But it would be a mistake to conclude that because the debates exist the problem is solved. Not only is it not solved but it may be obscured—because the most publicized fact is that we are permitted to cover debates between presidential candidates of the two major parties, and between vice presidential candidates. Beyond that, however, the existence of Section 315 prevents us from any special news coverage outside of regularly scheduled news and news-interview programs without the risk of supplying equal time to all the minor parties. The Federal Election Commission lists at least eighteen minority party presidential nominees and at least twenty-three independents.

And why does this archaic restriction stay with us? Well, first of all, it would take action by the Congress to eliminate it. And the conventional wisdom tells us that the incumbent—the present holder of office—loses some of his edge if his opposition receives significant exposure on television. That is because it is assumed the incumbent is better known than the opposition. Since the practical effect of [Section] 315 generally is to limit the exposure of all candidates, for all offices, we come up to a classic Catch 22 situation. The incumbent member of Congress is reluctant to vote for something—in this case the elimination of the equal-time requirement—that would allow his opposition to get wider attention. So Section 315 stays with us, and that situation is not likely to change in the foreseeable future.

Who loses? The public loses the opportunity to know about the contenders for their votes.

What is at stake here is not camera shots or studio lighting. It is a principle. The principle that a journalist must be free to do his job.

News coverage—if it is to meet its obligation to the public—cannot be controlled, directly or indirectly, by the people who are being covered, or by any intermediary.

If the 1976 debates are news events, they should be televised as news, by news professionals. Otherwise the whole principle of independent journalism is in jeopardy. That is an article of faith with NBC News, as it is with every responsible journalist. The public stands to get a better and more truthful view of events if the press functions with maximum freedom. When rules and formulas are imposed on news coverage the public is deprived of a constitutional right.

At the heart of all this is the continuing denial of full First Amendment status to broadcast news. Such restrictions as the equal-time rule and the Fairness Doctrine apply only to electronic journalists, and through them the journalists and the public are deprived of basic free-press rights. These rights can never be adequately restored unless broadcasters are given permanent relief from Section 315.

The lesson we keep learning over and over again in broadcast journalism is that you can't read the First Amendment two different ways. You can't have a news medium that operates half free and half controlled.

First, as I've suggested, restrictions have led to the creation of a news event that is being kept at arm's length from the news media themselves. And second, because the debates are based on a complicated FCC reinterpretation of the law, broadcasters could easily be caught up in a tangle of new equal-time demands by additional, minor candidates.

The problem I'm describing goes far beyond the question of the joint appearances of candidates Ford and Carter. What is more important is that our reporting on the entire electoral process is hampered. The result has been a lack of dimension in campaign coverage down the line, from the first New Hampshire primary to the eve of Election Day. Television and radio are severely inhibited in their ability to present the candidates directly, in the kind of journalistic context voters might find most useful.

It has been charged by some who fail to take the full picture into account that the network news organizations have not done a full and proper job in informing the public adequately on the candidates and the issues during presidential election campaigns. A prime example of this is in a recent book called *The Unseeing Eye* by two gentlemen from Syracuse University, Thomas Patterson and Robert McClure. My colleagues in NBC News have tried to read it with an objective eye, although we believe our medium does a far better job than the authors give it credit for. But what is most frustrating about such studies of television news is their failure to acknowledge the effects of equal-time restrictions on campaign coverage. As in criticizing the piano-playing of a man in a straitjacket, you have to make a few allowances.

I think we would all agree, however, that television—the medium most Americans rely on more than any other for news and insight—is not fulfilling its potential in election campaigns. That potential is considerable. And it goes well beyond the presentation of debates.

While this year NBC News has provided more campaign coverage than either of the other networks and more than at any time in its history, programs, outside of regular news and news-interview presentations, have had to avoid inclusion of the candidates themselves.

Without regulatory curbs, a variety of formats might be used to present the candidates and issues. For instance, NBC this year proposed to Congress and the FCC that, if Section 315 were suspended, we would offer four half-hours, free, to each of the major parties, in addition to the debates. We made similar proposals for every election going back to 1960. We would also have provided opportunity for candidates to appear in a series of campaign specials. Unfortunately, Section 315 has stayed in effect, and we could not follow through on this. I think the electoral process, and the public, were the losers.

But within the limitations imposed on us we do try, and try very hard. NBC has never mounted so large an effort of election reporting as in this Bicentennial year. Our coverage has stretched over a record number of thirty primary contests, two national conventions, and every step of the presidential campaign itself. We've had more special elec-tion-programming than ever before, and we've deployed a small army of reporters, technicians and producers along the campaign trail. We've also tried to put our reporting on a more scientific footing—with public polling, voter an-alysis and computer projections. Whatever works to inform and involve the voter—NBC is using it.

Beyond this, we're proposing reform in another area of political broadcasting—the sale of time to candidates. New election-financing rules—added to the increasing reliance on primary contests by candidates this year—have complicated the problem of finding space in the prime-time schedule to accommodate the candidates' needs.

We have suggested that before the 1980 Presidential pri-maries, the three television networks set aside an ample but fixed reserve of five-minute and half-hour periods in prime time. The national committees of the parties could serve as the clearinghouses for such a system, and some order can be brought to an area that's now very confused.

There are, of course, much larger questions concerning the electoral process that Americans should be thinking about. We hope to make a contribution there, too.

Next March, in Washington, before this election has faded from everyone's mind, NBC will conduct a major symposium on the whole electoral process and what needs to be done to make it more vital and effective. The meeting will be called the NBC Forum. It will be attended by polit-ical leaders, campaign specialists, former candidates, stu-dents of politics and journalists. It will study the most basic questions about our electoral process—from reforming the primary system to choosing a Vice President. And, of course, it won't ignore that perennial issue—the role of the media in elections. The Forum's findings will then be sum-marized and reported by NBC News on television and radio.

What I've been saying to you today can probably be summed up fairly simply: Television does serve the democratic process. It can do an even better job for the public and the voters of this country if given the same freedom to report on elections and politics as enjoyed by other media. We're trying to bring that about, and I hope that by the time you are broadcasting the news, we'll have made the job a little easier.

TELEVISED DEBATES [5]

LOWELL WEICKER JR. [6]

On September 10, 1976, Lowell P. Weicker Jr., Republican Senator from Connecticut, commented to his Senate colleagues about the forthcoming presidential debates, the first of which was held on September 23, 1976. His short speech is by no means a major senatorial effort, but he does set forth a point of view that needs to be considered. He advances a proposition fundamental to decision-making in a democracy: "the strength of America comes from her many voices." Probably few of Weicker's colleagues bothered to listen to him, for he spoke on a subject that did not touch them directly, yet his speech adds a dimension (not examined by Julian Goodman in the preceding speech) to the question of coverage for all presidential and vice presidential candidates.

Mr. President, on September 23, the American people will have the opportunity to see what our system of free elections is supposed to be all about. For the first time in sixteen years, major candidates for the presidency will meet, face to face, in televised debate.

The occasion has been heralded from all corners as a meaningful example of democracy at work—a long-awaited return to openness and candor between candidates for the highest honor Americans can bestow upon one of their own. For the first time in four elections, both the Republican and the Democratic nominees have decided to take the opposition seriously enough to tangle in open debate. The winner, we are told, will surely be the American voter.

Well, Mr. President, I would like to offer an alternate opinion: I think our major political parties are about to put one over on the voters. And the real significance of their act goes far beyond a single election day in November.

[5] Delivered in the United States Senate, September 10, 1976. Quoted from the *Congressional Record*, September 10, 1976, p S15545. Quoted by permission.
[6] For biographical note, see Appendix.

61

True, the up-coming debates may show the differences between President Ford and Jimmy Carter. But what they will also show are the Republican party and the Democratic party as the only alternatives for the American electorate. Through the magic of television, these two political organizations though increasingly irrelevant will take another giant step toward locking themselves in as America's only political parties. What neither the Constitution nor any law provides will now de facto be legislated into being by network television and the Democratic and Republican parties. What makes their action particularly ironic is that it is a minority imposing its will on the majority.

More Americans today identify themselves as independents than as either Democrat or Republican. I find it a sad commentary on the state of our political system that independent candidates for President are not afforded the same opportunity to present their views to the nation as are President Ford and Mr. Carter. Yes, I know how inconvenient such a theory is. But the Constitution of the United States is not an exercise in convenience, expediency or ease. It is a document meant for individuals, not "them" or "society" or the "greater good." When Article 1 states that "Congress shall make no law abridging the freedom of speech," I assume that means what it says both in content and intent. There is no exception made for non–Republicans or Democrats.

Our former colleague, Senator Eugene McCarthy, deserves to be heard, right along with the Republican and Democratic nominees. Actually I believe, though it has no bearing on my argument, that Gene McCarthy is living proof that you do not have to be a party big-wig to have ideas worth listening to. And, yes, for the chance to listen to Gene McCarthy, hearing Lester Maddox is the price we have to pay in a free society.

Mr. President, as party registrations dwindle party labels grow more meaningless and party activity more irrelevant. I find it frightening that our two major parties have stepped up their efforts to legislate themselves into perpetuity. The biggest step was the Federal Elections bill which this Congress passed. Its major feature was to assure the Republican and Democratic parties exclusive jurisdiction in picking the taxpayers' pockets for their campaigns. Independent candidates receive no matching funds to run their races.

Now it is television debates, and a not-so-subtle understanding between the participants, and network television that they will play only if the game is closed to everyone else.

What we have here is a severe case of political insecurity by two aging giants. That does not bother me, but using the Constitution of the United States as a bailing can for their sinking boats surely does.

Despite the television picture we will be offered on September 23, we on both sides of the aisle will do well to remember that our first obligation is to uphold the Constitution not our parties. And nowhere in that document are Democrats or Republicans granted special rights and privileges. In fact, the way both parties continue to feather their own nests while dodging the tough problems that face this country, they will be lucky to be around eight or twelve years from now—which seems to be the same fate we prescribe for anyone else's nonperformance in our society.

If the two parties continue to be irrelevant, self-serving legislation to cover up that deficiency is the last thing this nation needs.

As William V. Shannon said Monday in his perceptive New York *Times* column entitled, "The Third Man":

It is an unfavorable judgement on our federal and state laws that Eugene McCarthy should have to expend so much effort getting his name on the ballot and trying to get television coverage for his opinions. State electoral laws ought not to be a maze designed to baffle independent candidacies. If he is not permitted to participate in the Ford-Carter debates, television ought to afford him adequate time to present his views.

If independent voices and dissenting critics are to be heard in our ever bigger, more bureaucratized society, then these procedural issues of political access have to be resolved in favor of fairness and openness.

Mr. President, the strength of America comes from her many voices. Closing off America's voters to all but two voices and calling it a positive step is gutting the laws and spirits that made us great. If the Republican and Democratic parties want to retire and rest on their laurels, America should not. The future deserves better than the exclusive showing we will see two weeks from now.

IN PURSUIT OF EQUALITY

IN PURSUIT OF EQUALITY IN ACADEME:
NEW THEMES AND DISSONANT CHORDS [1]

ELEANOR HOLMES NORTON [2]

No person in the United States shall, on the basis of
sex, be excluded from participation in, be denied the benefits of, or be subjected to discrimination under any education program or activity receiving federal financial assistance (Title IX, Education Amendment of 1972).

The providing of equality of opportunity has caused college
administrators great concern. To even the balance of women and
blacks with present male faculty members has placed difficult
demands upon recruiters and upon systems of promotion. Before
the United States Senate, Senator Charles Percy (Republican,
Illinois) commented in 1974: "Barriers that confront women on
the educational ladder range from female stereotyping in grade
school, to the exclusion of girls and women from classes and
programs designed for men, to the relegation of women to low-
paying, low-level positions in schools and colleges." The *Equal
Rights Monitor* (March/April, 1977) reports: "Women comprise
only 20.6 percent of faculty members of four-year colleges. . . .
Women hold only 9.4 percent of the full professorships but make
up 43.5 percent of positions at the beginning instructor level."

The program planners of the American Association for
Higher Education could not have found a better person to discuss the theme Quality and Equality in Higher Education than
Eleanor Holmes Norton, then Commissioner of Human Rights
for the City of New York and recently appointed by President
Carter to head the Equal Employment Opportunity Commission.
On March 7, 1976, she spoke to the opening session of the thirty-
first national conference of that organization meeting at the Conrad Hilton Hotel in Chicago. The audience was made up of college and university administrators—including presidents, deans,

[1] Delivered before the opening session of the thirty-first National Conference
on Higher Education, at the Conrad Hilton Hotel, Chicago, March 7, 1976. Published in a slightly different form in *Individualizing the System*, edited by Dyck-
man W. Vermile, Jossey-Bass, San Francisco, 1976, p 200-11. Quoted by permission of the author and the publisher.

[2] For biographical note, see Appendix.

and departmental chairmen—graduate students, and a few government and foundation officials.

At the close of her speech she drew a standing ovation.

Commissioner Norton, a black lawyer, has been a civil rights activist since her student days at Antioch College. She has been described as "a slender woman of just over medium height, with a warm, open manner and a rich, strong voice that breaks frequently into a relaxed laugh" (Philadelphia *Bulletin*, November 24, 1974). She was a staff member of the 1963 March on Washington and in 1964 a counsel to the Mississippi Freedom Democratic party. She has attracted national attention for her activities in New York City in fighting job and sex discrimination.

Ladies and Gentlemen:

I knew I was speaking before a group of hardy academic souls when I learned that you unfailingly come to Chicago each March for this conference, apparently willingly, choosing it out of all the more gentle places in other parts of the country. Were you from some other sectors of our society, you might not be so hipped on Chicago. You would alternate between Puerto Rico and Miami. Anyway, I am pleased as a dyed-in-the-wool New Yorker to welcome you to Chicago.

A new equality has emerged during the past twenty years. It has been very much discussed but too little analyzed. It has been negatively associated with everything from the development of permissiveness to the demise of law and order. Its positive accreditations have sometimes been similarly exaggerated, as the use of the language of liberation to describe significant but modest moves toward equality would suggest. It has annoyed or exhilarated every significant and most insignificant parts of our society, not the least of them higher education.

The emergence of black people out of the shadows as darkies and into the light as blacks is of course the throbbing center of the newest impulse toward equality. But the nation is still unraveling its oldest, most torturous, most redundant riddle—the settlement of its black people. For they, alone among America's immigrants, remain unsettled after three hundred years. Over these centuries they moved from slave plantations to rural hovels until they emerged in the twentieth century as a profoundly urban people still searching for their place in America. What changed slowest about them was their status in America. In a land where mobility seemed mandated and came to all but the damned, America's dark-skinned immigrants remain at the bottom. Only in the past two decades, beginning with the *Brown* decision, has there been any serious challenge to the permanency of the subterranean status of America's blacks and its other people of color.

So elastic was this new equality that it readily reached to accommodate women, the nation's unequal majority, as well. Following the pattern of the black revolution, women began rapidly redefining the meaning of equality for themselves and thus for all of us in the 1970s. Should they fully succeed they could by the force of their numbers and the inherent radicalism of their demands cause society itself to make fundamental alterations.

But the open struggle of blacks for equality influenced many more than those who saw themselves as similarly situated. The original social energy of the period in which we still live derives from the civil rights movement. The anti-war movement, the women's rights movement, the anti-poverty movement, the struggles of other minorities—all patterned themselves in one fashion or another on the extraordinarily fertile civil rights struggle.

Most of the developments toward deeper equality took shape and substance from the 1960s, a period characterized by the upset of social convention and injustice. The decade of the sixties was in deep reaction to the spirit of the fifties, a decade rooted more in the notion that all men should be alike than that they should be equal. The young people of the sixties were a quintessential movement generation. They were as shaped by social movements as the generation of the fifties was shaped by none.

Some changes that characterize the new equality appear

fairly permanent. The black struggle for equality has changed America as much as it has changed the status of blacks. White Americans today are the first white people in the nation's history to be decisively influenced in their values by the experience, aspirations, and actions of black Americans. Martin Luther King Jr. influenced America as much as John F. Kennedy. Aretha Franklin and James Brown shaped the style of this period in the way that Dinah Shore and Bing Crosby influenced their parents' youth.

Such changes may be new, but they emerge from a special historic context. The recent vintage of changes in matters of equality sometimes serves to obscure the fact of a much longer American obsession with this subject. Historians may differ as to when to date its beginnings. But the nationalization of the anti-slavery controversy with the Missouri Compromise surely demarks a point when slavery and thus equality became truly national concerns tied to the destiny of the nation itself. At least since 1820, then, I think it fair to say that Americans have had an unparalleled and unceasing struggle with themselves over the meaning and the virtue of equality.

For no other people has equality required such sustained attention for so long a time. Nowhere else in the world has the struggle over this single question been so intense, so dynamic, so costly.

I would include within this more than 150-year period not only the perplexing and omnipresent struggle of black men and women. For mounted on the same canvas are the collages of others, including the old women's-suffrage movement, the women's-equality movement of today, and the largely successful struggle of European immigrants for inclusion on terms of equality and mobility. The very diversity of the actors who have played out equality themes in America has contributed to the preoccupation of Americans with this subject.

The American experience with equality has been both tortured and exhilarating. At the most promising end of the scale, successive waves of poor immigrants—most entering as illiterate peasants—found spectacular economic success in one or two generations, a phenomenal mobility unprecedented in world history. Somewhere in between are white women who, with the right to vote, won a new sense of themselves after a long struggle. While their transformation in equality terms is incomplete and disappointing, no one can doubt what the past fifty years have done to make the American woman more equal, both in her home and in her transformed role as member of the workforce. At the low end of the scale, the national experience with black people has been a unique tragedy, characterized first by sustained oppression and then by furtive progress. Still the past two decades have raised uncommon hopes and produced unprecedented gains. At the very least, black people have come from psychological depths to which it would seem impossible to return.

In any case Americans have had more diverse and concentrated experience with the dynamics of equality than any other people in the world. This has given America the opportunity to disproportionately influence the very meaning of the word. The American experience has done as much to define equality for the world as the Russian Revolutionary period did to give reality to Marxism.

Examples of American leadership on matters of equality, leadership often carved out of painful experience, are legion. The choice of Martin Luther King Jr. for world recognition as recipient of the Nobel Peace Prize in 1964 did not come because of his leadership of an indigenous freedom movement in the United States. King's world status derives from the same process that made world and not merely national leaders of Gandhi and Lenin. All staged essentially national movements with such universal force and applicability, that they moved men and women across the face of the earth. King made the idea of racial equality plainer to millions than it had ever been before, just as Gandhi moved peasants everywhere to demand freedom from colonialism.

One could cite other examples of American pace setting in the conception of equality. The women's movement appears better developed in this country than in most others. The French have a new cabinet post for the *condition feminine* but underdeveloped notions of feminism and no strong activist movement. Russian and other East European women have won significant access to male jobs but very little change in sex roles. By contrast, American women, with historically better developed notions of equality to work with, are pursuing change in magnificent proportions from carefully circumscribed issues such as equal employment and universal child care to weighty philosophical issues whose resolution could virtually redefine womanhood and remake entire areas of human experience.

All of these developments toward greater equality in America have been influenced in no small measure by American higher education, both in its functional educational role and in its role as a social force. But Academe, like most other sections of our society, is experiencing some difficulty today, when pressure for equality implementation has succeeded the simple demand for common justice. New and more complicated equality themes have replaced easier notions of simple justice from the days of "Freedom Now."

Thus, you do well to hold a conference concerned with equality and quality in what appears to be a congenial and truly searching atmosphere. I think it fair to say that in a very real sense the country has traditionally depended on American higher education, more than on most others, for leadership on issues of equality. But in recent years there have been some uncharacteristically discordant chords emanating from Academe on matters of equality, seeming to challenge the applicability of equality principles to the university setting. These arguments have been made in such a way as to undermine the preeminent place of the American university as a locus for pushing the society toward the realization of its own highest ideals.

I do not fault academic voices for their criticism of this

or that government approach to affirmative action in university employment, for example. There is, I assure you, much room for criticism. Moreover the university is in a position to offer the most useful of criticism, because of its own research and scholarly functions. Affirmative action should not be exempt from criticism from Academe simply because the university is affected.

Rather I would argue just the opposite: that the academic community is in a unique position to contribute to the perfection of techniques for achieving equality but has inexplicably hung back from this natural function in recent years. This can be seen both in areas where the university has some self-interest and in areas where it does not.

Let me cite just one where universities themselves are not implicated, simply for the purpose of making my point about the university lag in contributing to the resolution of increasingly difficult equality issues in America today. Consider busing, a technique encountering deepening trouble and unpopularity throughout the country. When Professor James Coleman recently suggested that busing had spurred white flight from the cities and had thus hurt school integration, something of a furor developed. This deepened when it was learned that the cities he had studied had indeed experienced flight but not busing. Many who believe in school integration now simply discount Dr. Coleman's view as that of just one more turn-coat liberal adversary to integration. This, of course, is unfair to Professor Coleman. Busing, like any controversial technique, needs criticism if we are to have any hope of making improvements. But in the context of today's chilled climate for racial equality, a finding that comes out of a decidedly negative context will only contribute to controversy. The need is not so much for less criticism of the mechanisms of integration as it is for a more forthright search for answers to complicated new issues that arise as we untangle our tortured racial past.

Indeed the need for clear analysis suggesting pathways to permanent equality solutions is especially great today, par-

ticularly in light of the inadequacy of a number of techniques in use. But when the thrust is one of complaint,
rather than of searching—that a technique, busing for example, is not working, without more—many hear only the
sound of retreat. If not busing, what is proposed? In a country where racial degradation and separation have been the
rule, few blacks are prepared to consider arguments based
on the utility of various approaches to equality—not when
whites have so often found the entire exercise of equality
unuseful. This may not be a wholly rational response, but it
is understandable. Professor Coleman's conclusions concerning busing might have been received differently had they
arisen within a more balanced study. In the absence of a
committed search for alternatives, civil rights advocates feel
they will be a part of their own undoing if they acquiesce in
doubts about busing or other integration techniques.

Who is in the best position to search for alternatives to
this troublesome issue? Politicians who find the issue especially treacherous in the political marketplace? The government which feels the day-by-day pressure from both
sides? Judges sworn to expand constitutional principle and
ignore popular reaction? None is in a better position than
the university where detachment and time are afforded to
think through society's most difficult problems—from cures
for diseases to, yes, school integration. How are we to account therefore for the scant study of the actual experience
of children in integrated settings, except for the search for
magical improvement in test scores many somehow expected
school integration to produce? There is a danger that one
hopeful technique, the magnet school—one with special
features or additional resources designed to attract a bal-
lanced role-mix—will fall by the way because of lack of
study of what specific features make a school able to attract
white students in this way. I have seen such magnets thrown
together so carelessly that they fail, giving the hopeful magnet concept a bad name as just one more failed integration
technique. And I have seen others that succeed brightly.

One would think that some professor would be busily cataloging success and failure factors in magnet schools and by this time would be well on his way to developing a success model. My own Commission, hard pressed by budget cutbacks, is considering undertaking such a study in the absence of this kind of assistance from the academic community to meet urgent problems of school integration.

Busing is only one of a litany of issues produced by the new complexities of race, ethnicity, and sex in America where the need for thoughtful study is as clear as the neglect of scholarly attention. Just to mention two others among the most serious: The conflict between the values of seniority and affirmative action, a most difficult question, is greatly in need of the best conceptual treatment. Another is the awesomely complicated question of encouraging racially and economically diverse cities in the face of white flight, the flight of other middle income people, and the resulting catastrophic effect on the viability of the American city itself. Both of these are issues on which my small government agency, without a single Ph.D., has been struggling without federal or academic leadership.

Why problems of such magnitude have inspired so little academic attention is not altogether clear. But this failure on large issues of equality has not helped to create an affirmative and hospitable atmosphere once these issues have come closer to home.

And they have come home to roost in Academe on both faculty and student selection. The faculty discrimination issues have provoked much more hostile reaction from administrators and faculty than student selection matters, although the issues are at least of equal moment. The society has at least as great a stake in fair student selection as in fair faculty selection. Of course, the matter of self-interest is, I think you will agree, a bit clearer in one than in the other. In any case, the cries from college and university presidents and professors, almost all of them white men, have not been received by the public as disinterested laments.

I do not mean to imply that their points of criticism are totally without merit. What I am saying is that they have no right to ask what amounts to an exemption for the university from many of the procedures of the civil rights laws. While today most academic institutions have found their way toward a posture of compliance, the early outcries, especially from the university presidents, called for a virtual exemption of colleges and universities from many of the only effective procedures that have been developed, all of which apply to every other large employer in the country. These techniques include an evaluation of confidential personnel records, a matter not without difficulty, but one also not beyond the reach of those interested in compliance with the civil rights laws. And goals and timetables for rectifying exclusion within universities have also been subject to special displeasure. This issue, which continues to plow discord in Academe, is also capable of resolution if compliance rather than avoidance is the goal.

The fact is that the blame for the way the controversy between the universities and HEW developed belongs with both sides. When compliance was first attempted, the universities responded like wounded deer, the victims of a predator that did not understand the sensitivity of the beast. Its traditional strong concern for equality was not summoned in this, its own personal equality crisis. No galaxy of professors presented themselves as a technical task force to bring some reason into the process. The university chose noncompliance until persistence by the federal government appeared to destroy that option.

In the same way HEW, which had seen the face of recalcitrance before, identified this as just another garden variety. The agency was mindful that women professors had filed a massive class action against the entire university community, to prod the Department into a more forthright discharge of its anti-discrimination duties. In this atmosphere the question of whether some serious work might be done by the Department to adapt its procedures to college and university employment systems did not arise until negotiations occurred, often only after painful confrontation and then, at least until recently, on an *ad hoc* rather than a systematic and comprehensive basis.

I believe that a sound case can be made that universities constitute a special case when it comes to anti-discrimination enforcement and therefore are in need of special assistance and perhaps even a system of race and sex analysis and implementation of remedies attuned to the peculiar contours of the university work place. As a technician with some experience in this field, I accept the view that factors which in other situations must be rigidly controlled, such as credentialism and broad discretion to evaluate a candidate, must have fuller sway in the selection of faculty. Moreover, I believe this need not lead to more lenient application of the anti-discrimination laws to universities than to other employers, a wholly unfair and unacceptable result. By not looking at the university system in this particularized way, HEW may have sown the seeds that have made enforcement so tough and controversial in colleges and universities.

But if the government should have developed and provided better technical assistance to the universities, it is universities themselves, which, ironically are the richest resource for creating the appropriate technology. No other employer in the nation was in a position to influence government equal opportunity policy in the way the university was and is. By merely playing the role society expects of it, Academe had within its hands the power to shut down the controversy over the procedures of compliance and, through research and scholarly study, submit alternatives.

I am not suggesting that the university might have designed its own mode of compliance to equal opportunity laws. I am saying that by regarding the matter of compliance adversarily and not as an honest question of considerable technical difficulty, the university defaulted in its commitment to equality and encouraged needless and harmful controversy. No group of professors undertook to look at these as serious questions for study. Instead some formed themselves into a committee to oppose affirmative action.

One professor has authored a recent book designed to show that court decisions and other government actions to enforce the civil rights laws have themselves discriminated against the majority, a work whose deficiencies begin with the author's failure to read and digest the relevant court decisions or to understand the basic law of remedies in our system of jurisprudence. Nowhere in all of corporate America, with its historic lack of identification with equality and association with prejudice, has so negative a development toward equality emerged. It has fallen to the university to speak for the recalcitrant employer.

Problems of equality in the university promise to accentuate, not diminish in the years ahead. While faculties doubled in the 1960s, with 30,000 new hires a year, in the 1980s only 6,000 new hires annually are expected, a replacement rate that itself may diminish, as the years of fantastic expansion are followed not even by stabilization, but, as likely as not, by retrenchment. Last month the U.S. Office of Education reported that in 1975 faculty women lost ground in both salary increase and rank. According to the report, "The average salaries of men continue to exceed the average salaries of women at every academic rank and at every institutional level, in both publicly and privately controlled institutions." If the university is to avoid becoming a haven for racial and sex discord, it must summon its own best traditions, marshall its decided skill, and absorb itself in designing strategies for genuine equality in Academe.

In the same way student selection policies need urgent attention. If student admission procedures have upset administrators and professors less than faculty selection, they have been of considerable concern in the society-at-large. Again, part of the blame rests squarely with government. Colleges and universities have been left almost totally to their own devices in designing techniques for the admission of disadvantaged minority students. The government encouraged the opening of opportunities but, as in the case of university affirmative action, provided no technical assistance.

The result was the *DeFunis* case and a number of others like it. These cases demonstrate that universities had considerably more good will than expertise in criteria for evaluating disadvantaged minority students, who have been historically excluded from their student population. That good will has substantially diminished in the face of budgetary cutbacks and the controversy emanating from these very cases. But the problem will remain until someone decides to consider it an issue worthy of serious research and study. As with affirmative action technology, I cannot avoid asking again, who is in a better position than academicians themselves.

Neither the university nor the government has chosen to move toward rational problem solving here either. Instead court cases continue to make this explosive issue more so. The adversarial route has been chosen over the scholarly search.

Here the government is particularly at fault, for there has been a persuasive appeal for help on this matter before HEW for almost two years. After the inconclusive Supreme Court decision in the *DeFunis* case I talked with the heads of six national racial and ethnic organizations, all with headquarters in New York, who had been on opposite sides of the case. The following letter to then HEW Secretary Caspar Weinberger resulted:

Dear Dr. Weinberger:
While the undersigned organizations have taken varying positions on the *DeFunis* case, we have, over the years worked closely in support of civil rights and human freedom.

We all recognize that the process of creating affirmative action is not an exact science. It is only in the past few years that the nation has begun the development of procedures for dismantling discrimination.

All of us wish to avoid polarization. We agree that a primary goal for all of us is the elimination of all forms of discrimination and the establishment of affirmative actions and processes that will provide equal opportunity within our constitutional framework.

Since the issues raised by the *DeFunis* case remain, we believe that an early response from HEW, within whose jurisdiction such matters lie, is indicated. We are therefore requesting that you direct the issuance of non-discriminatory guidelines clarifying how educational institutions can best develop appropriate tools for special efforts to recruit persons from previously excluded groups.

This letter was signed by the heads of the Anti-Defamation League of B'nai Brith, the American Jewish Committee, the American Jewish Congress, the NAACP, the National Urban League, and the Puerto Rican Legal Defense and Educational Fund.

Mr. Weinberger reacted immediately and a departmental study and letter of guidelines to college and university presidents were promised. Over a year later, when Dr. Weinberger was about to resign, I wrote to remind him that all were awaiting the promised guidance and was assured that the matter would be carried on by his successor in the department. Now almost another year has passed with no resolution of these issues.

This is inexcusable neglect from the federal government. The standards are theirs to give. Still government default need not have been decisive on the question. The knowledge and skills to develop the fair admission devices are found in special abundance among various disciplines in the very universities that now must commit resources instead to fighting court cases. Once again Academe has lost its way on issues that were thought to be of special concern.

In a very special way the country needs you who teach and administer higher education today. Rearrangements among the races and sexes and classes appear too complicated for many. The swirling events of our time seem to many not the inevitable content of modern change but a signal of endemic instability in American life. The line between rapid, dynamic change and meandering, perplexing instability has always been thin. But that line is not drawn entirely by events. It is drawn also by those who shape and react to events.

At such times, education is or should be a valuable hedge against bewilderment and panic. More than most Americans, educational leaders understand the reasons for the fear of change. After all, until the twentieth century most of the world's people lived virtually changeless lives. Change was a matter of the seasons or of youth mellowing into old age, which often came by forty. Change itself is a twentieth century phenomenon. Change has made all our lives more difficult. But it has also made them more rewarding. We are richer but we are also more burdened.

I would be the first to agree that higher education cannot and should not always pursue the utilitarian. You are not society's anointed problem-solvers. But you have always ventured special concern for equality in America. It is time to step forward once again. Someone needs to stand with both reason and justice. If not you, who?

WOMEN AND EQUALITY UNDER THE LAW [3]

ELIZABETH HOLTZMAN [4]

In spite of opposition and reverses women have continued their battle for equal rights. While the Equal Rights Amendment (ERA) has been passed by thirty-five states to date, women are still far behind men in holding public office. For instance, at present seventeen women serve in the House of Representatives —one fewer than in the previous session—and three of them come from Maryland. No woman is now a United States Senator. Only two states have elected a woman as governor: Connecticut and Washington. In the cabinet are Juanita Kreps, Secretary of Commerce, and Patricia Harris, Secretary of Housing and Urban Development, but a fall 1976 estimate showed that across the nation women held between 4 and 7 percent of all public jobs; they occupied about 10 percent of 1300 state-wide elective and cabinet positions; numbered about 8 percent of the 7,500 state legislators (*Wall Street Journal*, October 21, 1976).

One person well qualified to speak on the subject of equal rights for women is Representative Elizabeth Holtzman, who addressed the Women in the Law Conference at Madison, Wisconsin, on March 26, 1977. For her audience of female lawyers she developed the proposition, "I would . . . caution you against putting all your eggs in a litigation basket, especially one that seems to be full of holes." In support of her proposition of policy she developed a need contention based on solid evidence and then presented a definite plan of action. The student of argumentation and debate will find here a model speech that lends itself to briefing.

A leader in the struggle for equal rights, Holtzman has become known as an outstanding liberal legislator. At the age of thirty-one she won her seat, surprisingly, by defeating eighty-four-year-old Emanuel Cellers, a congressman for forty-nine years in the New York Sixteenth Congressional District that is predominantly liberal, Jewish, and middle class. One of her criticisms of her opponent was his resistance to equal rights. As a freshman Representative she won recognition from television viewers as one of the two women members (Barbara Jordan was

[3] Delivered at Women in the Law Conference, University of Wisconsin, Madison, March 26, 1977.
[4] For biographical note, see Appendix.

the other) of the House Judiciary Committee that considered impeachment of Richard M. Nixon. She frequently speaks out for equal rights (*Biography News*, March 1974) in the House and before outside groups.

Last year our country celebrated its two hundredth birthday. At least by then, and surely by now, we should have been able to say that women in the United States have achieved equality under the law. But America's failure to make good on its promise to more than half of its people —a promise of human dignity and individual worth implicit in the Declaration of Independence and the Constitution—is why we are all here at this conference: to understand how we can use our experience, our intelligence and our determination more effectively to remedy the wrong that has been done to women for far too long.

As lawyers, most of you have been trained to look to the courts for solutions to injustice. But this bias—which views litigation as the primary solution to our problems—needs to be corrected. The record of our courts on women's rights is not one that justifies that kind of confidence. The Supreme Court—which in the nineteenth century closed its own doors to women lawyers—took more than one hundred years to decide that the Fourteenth Amendment even applied to women. The court still has not gone far enough. It continues to refuse to rule that sex discrimination is automatically questionable and that classification by sex is automatically suspect.

Indeed, earlier this month, four Supreme Court justices proclaimed that the Fourteenth Amendment prohibited only "invidious" sex discrimination—in other words the plain ordinary garden variety of paternalistic, misogynistic sex discrimination is all right. It seems that all the justices agree with this position since just this week they unanimously approved a law that discriminates on the basis of sex.

Not only has the Supreme Court withheld the full protection of the Constitution from women, but it has even refused to extend to us the explicit benefits of statutory law. The *Gilbert* decision, which claims that discrimination against pregnant women is not sex discrimination, should give us all pause in thinking about the Supreme Court as a vindicator of our rights. And we thought they were for motherhood! A court composed of nine women could never arrive at a decision that is so oblivious to biological reality.

In addition, the court's recent restrictions on standing, class actions and suits to enforce civil rights under section 1983 will make it extremely difficult for women's rights advocates to end systematic sex discrimination through court suits.

I would thus caution you against putting all your eggs in a litigation basket, especially one that seems to be so full of holes.

But that does not mean that women trained in the law should despair about using their special expertise effectively. There is an enormous role for women lawyers to play in formulating social policy, in shaping the laws that govern our conduct, in removing sex stereotypes from our laws, and in seeing that the laws on the books are enforced fairly.

We simply cannot afford to overlook the Congress or the Executive Branch of government in our efforts to improve the status of women. That is not to say that we can expect an unblemished record of performance from them either. After all, when the Supreme Court declared that women had a constitutional right to an abortion, it was the Congress (in an act of cowardice and callousness) that tried to restrict the availability of that right for poor women. Similarly, the Executive Branch has systematically failed to enforce many of the antidiscrimination laws on the books.

We have to recognize that we cannot expect real responsiveness from any federal institutions unless and until women fully participate in them. This means we have to liberate the Supreme Court, the Senate, the presidency, as well as increase the number of women who presently serve in Congress, on the federal bench, and in executive agencies.

It is dismaying to realize that although the first woman was elected to Congress in 1916, today we have only eighteen women in the House and none in the Senate. In fact, we seem to be going backwards. Four prior Congresses had more women members than the one that just began.

In the entire history of this country, we have had only nine women on the federal bench and five cabinet secretaries. The first and only woman US attorney was appointed by Woodrow Wilson.

Obviously one of our central and urgent priorities must be changing these statistics, but we can't just sit back and wait for the situation to improve. We must move to increase the numbers of women in our government and simultaneously prod our institutions to take action on a host of crucial women's issues.

That is not as impossible as it seems. Congress, for example, has acted on some issues in the past. Although prompted by southerners who hoped to torpedo the Civil Rights Act of 1964, Congress enacted Title VII which bans discrimination against women in employment. It adopted the Equal Pay Act mandating equal pay for equal work. In 1972, Congress passed the Equal Rights Amendment and called for its ratification by the states. Since then it has prohibited federally funded educational institutions from discriminating against women in employment and from segregating sports or other programs on the basis of sex. It has barred sex discrimination in credit and in the administration of crime control, public works, and public employment programs. It has provided a tax credit for day care expenses. It has opened the military academies to women, funded programs to combat sex stereotyping in careers, paid for the creation of non-sexist educational materials, set up a National Institute for Rape, developed programs to encourage women to enter scientific careers, and covered domestic workers under Social Security and the minimum wage laws.

While this list may sound impressive, don't be deceived. Given the seriousness of the problem and the pervasiveness of sex stereotypes in our laws and social programs, it represents only a small step toward what is needed.

First, we need to change the laws that assume women are dependent, homebound creatures—that thus discriminate against working women, and often against men, and actually provide no reliable protection to women either.

The Social Security laws are profoundly discriminatory. Drafted in the 1930s, they assume that most women will not work and that most men will. Consequently, they provided that women can automatically derive benefits from their husbands' earnings, but husbands cannot automatically derive benefits from their wives' work. The law also permitted a widow with young children to derive benefits for both her children and herself from her husband's work but allowed a widower to receive benefits based on his wife's earnings only for his children and not for himself. These provisions were stricken by the Supreme Court.

But there are other inequities remaining. Most married women who work receive the same benefits that they would have if they had never worked a single day. The reason for this is that most women who work earn less than men, as a result of discrimination and restrictions on career choices. Since benefit levels are geared to earnings, most wives receive their benefits on the basis of their husband's earnings. They receive no benefit at all from the Social Security taxes they pay. This is unfair to working women.

In addition, since the Social Security law assumes that wives will be dependent, we would expect homemakers to receive reliable protection. That is not, in fact, the case.

Homemakers receive no independent Social Security credit for their contribution to the family. Moreover, their Social Security benefits are conditioned upon the continued favor of their husbands, since a woman divorced before she has been married twenty years has no claim to benefits on her husband's record.

Our tax laws also reflect a bias about women that needs to be changed. Where both husband and wife work, they pay a severe tax penalty for their marriage, while a couple where the husband works but wife doesn't, pay no tax penalty.

The much maligned welfare system is also, I believe, a product of stereotyped thinking about women. The premise underlying welfare is that a man is always the breadwinner —that a mother cannot be expected to support herself and her family. Therefore, in most states, welfare automatically gets cut off if the husband is present—even if he can't find a job. Similarly there is neither sufficient training for real jobs nor adequate day care so welfare mothers can find work. Our welfare system causes families to break up and makes the ideology of a woman's dependency a self-fulfilling nightmare.

Second, we need to offer some real help to America's working women and those who want the dignity of work and economic independence.

The fight for equal pay and equal job opportunities is far from won. In fact, the earning gap between men and women has widened in the past twenty years. As just one measure of how far we have to go, even if 50 percent of all new faculty members who are hired in our nation's colleges were women, by 1990 women would still only constitute a mere 30 percent of our nation's college faculties.

In the past few years, we have seen substantial gains in job opportunities for women through affirmative action recruitment. These gains are threatened, however, by a lagging economy, since women, as the last hired, are likely to be the first fired. Solutions to this complicated problem must be found.

Federal employment and training programs need to be redesigned and refocused so that they benefit more women.

The first thing that should be changed is their name. It is no accident they are called "Manpower Programs" since they are heavily weighted toward construction and public works jobs that are more likely to employ men.

We should experiment with flex-time and part-time employment.

Adequate day care is needed if women are to be able to work. President Nixon vetoed a day care bill calling it "family weakening." Although Mr. Nixon has gone, Congress still refuses to pass comprehensive day care legislation. It simply won't come to grips with the reality that there are more than 61 million children with working mothers and that almost 18 million of those children are under six. We also need to make sure that funds for day care actually go to benefit the children. Recent investigations in New York City revealed much of the money was going to pay inflated rents to politically connected real estate speculators.

We also need quickly to pass legislation reversing the *Gilbert* decision so that pregnant workers will not be singled out for discrimination in matters like hiring, firing, and insurance. The Supreme Court left pregnant women vulnerable to discrimination. Action is underway, and just three and one half months after the decision, bills have been introduced in both houses of Congress with the support of a broad coalition of labor, women, and civil rights groups.

Third, we need some protection for women who have chosen to be full-time homemakers. Homemakers left single by divorce or by the death of their husbands need help in reentering the job market when their skills are rusty and so much time has passed that they face not only possible sex discrimination but age discrimination as well.

There must be ways to shelter, counsel, and assist battered wives who live in daily fear for their own and their children's safety but are afraid to leave because they do not have the economic means to make it on their own. There must be a change in our laws on every level to protect a woman from rape and brutalization whether from her husband or otherwise.

There must be effective measures to enforce child support orders so families do not become destitute when fathers desert them.

Congress can provide only part of the answer to the problems of women. The Executive Branch must also be monitored and pressured.

A starting point has to be the Equal Employment Opportunity Commission. Our mechanism for enforcing laws against employment discrimination is in disarray. A recent report on the EEOC revealed that it had a backlog of 127,800 discrimination charges including some that were nine years old. In the cases it acted on, half were closed without investigation.

Plainly, past Administrations had no interest in seeking effective enforcement of the laws. The failure to enforce our laws against sex discrimination makes a mockery of them. This has to be changed.

Our other effort must be to ensure that the executive agencies will promulgate enforcement regulations that do not undermine the intent of good legislation. The Federal Reserve Board—which has no women on it—tried to gut the Equal Credit Act with weakening regulations. The Board was stopped—mostly by the efforts of women's groups and a coalition of congresswomen—but this will be a continuing problem.

Revising our Social Security, tax and welfare laws; making day care readily available; seeing that the Equal Employment Opportunity Commission works—all of these are complex tasks. It is no easy matter to remove the old inequities without creating new ones.

This is where you come in. We need your talents and ability to help us fashion legislative remedies to these problems and to myriads of others as well.

You may ask, "Why is my help needed?" You probably

will be surprised to learn that legislators don't have the
staff assistance and the expertise they need to deal with all
of the legislative tasks they face, much less to deal systematically with problems affecting women. For example, almost
every congresswoman has relied on outside experts to criti-
cize, to draft or to propose new legislative solutions on
women's issues. Your willingness to work for public officials,
at every level of government, on a voluntary basis or otherwise could make an enormous difference in the quality of
the solutions and how fast they come.

Give us the benefit of your experience with the various
kinds of problems that women around this country confront
and suggest solutions. In your law practices, you encounter
women from different geographic areas, different economic
and age groups, and different personal situations. You can
educate us about women's problems that have been ignored
or misunderstood.

Finally, you have to become political in the broadest
sense of that term. Learn how this system works and make
it work for you.

Start by confronting your own representatives on issues
of key concern to women and then link hands with or form
organizations of women to act as broad-based pressure
groups.

Lobbying can make an enormous difference. The
women's movement has unfortunately still not learned to
use the technique as effectively as possible. In the last Congress, we were able to win when women's groups lobbied
well and lost when they didn't.

Thus, when a congressman first tried to block a ban on
separate physical education programs for boys and girls,
raising hysterical objections that we would have topless
bathing suits in high school swimming classes and income-
producing sports would be destroyed, his amendment passed
by one vote. Women's groups mounted an extremely well-
organized intensive countereffort and, two days later, the
amendment was defeated by thirty-seven votes.

Unfortunately, we didn't do as well in preventing the passage of the Hyde Amendment which prohibits the use of Medicaid funds for abortions. The major concern of most congressmen and senators, expressed privately, was that they would not be reelected if they voted in favor of abortion. Women's groups were unable to mount a successful lobbying effort to convince members of Congress that an anti-abortion vote could have reelection consequences as well.

Prospects this year are even worse. The Hyde Amendment will almost undoubtedly be included as an integral part of the relevant bills and only a massive grass roots lobbying effort by women will be able to stop this from happening.

The failure of women's groups to mobilize may mean that poor women in this country will be deprived of the right to have an abortion. Moreover, even if we are saved from the Hyde Amendment by the courts, its repeated passage in the Congress will encourage advocates of a constitutional amendment.

The same failure to mobilize grass roots support has stalled quick ratification of the Equal Rights Amendment. Women's rights groups have permitted a small vocal minority to capture the attention of state legislators and to convince these men, who are all too eager to listen, that this minority represents the views of most women.

The problem perhaps is that many women are unaccustomed to using the political process, to writing representatives, visiting them, and making their concerns heard. Women like you who have had the benefit of a legal education, who are articulate and well trained, have a special responsibility to help organize other women and to give voice to the concerns of the majority of women on the Equal Rights Amendment and other issues.

But, it is not enough for you to lobby, organize, speak out, and help congresswomen get elected. Join the process itself. We need you in Congress, we need you in the Senate, we need you in the city halls, we need you in the governors' mansions.

Remember the congressional accomplishments I mentioned earlier. In almost every case, the prime mover was a woman. If there were more of us, just think what we could achieve!

Don't have any hesitation about your own abilities to get elected. If you need any inspiration, just look at the men who already hold office.

That's how I got started. When I was working in New York City Hall, I looked around one day and said if *they* can get elected, so can I. And so can you.

DeTocqueville observed more than one hundred years ago that America was run by its lawyers. That is still the case, and perhaps that is one of our problems. But as long as it *is* the case, there is no reason that more of those lawyers shouldn't be women.

Much has been accomplished but much remains to be done. We are in much better position now to reach our objectives than ever before. I look out on an audience like this and see so many able and talented and articulate women, and I know that we will succeed if we can learn to work together and if we just try.

SOLUTIONS TO MALNUTRITION AND SQUALOR

SEARCHING FOR NEW SOLUTIONS TO POVERTY [1]

ROBERT S. McNAMARA [2]

If we look about the world today realistically, it is evident that the desire for . . . a more just and reasonable equality of opportunity among individuals, both within nations and between nations is becoming a major concern of our time. . . .

This broad thrust is growing more insistent today in all nations. It is searching for new solutions to the intolerable problems of poverty.

The per capita incomes of the more than one billion human beings in the poorest countries have nearly stagnated over the past decade. In statistical terms they have risen only about two dollars a year: from $130 in 1965, to $150 in 1975.

But what is beyond the power of any set of statistics to illustrate is the inhuman degradation the vast majority of these individuals are condemned to because of poverty.

Malnutrition saps their energy, stunts their bodies, and shortens their lives. Illiteracy darkens their minds, and forecloses their futures. Simple, preventable diseases maim and kill their children. Squalor and ugliness pollute and poison their surroundings.

The miraculous gift of life itself, and all its intrinsic potential—so promising and rewarding for us—is eroded and reduced for them to a desperate effort to survive.

These sentences concluded an earlier address that Robert S. McNamara, president of the World Bank Group, delivered to the board of governors in their meeting in Manila, October 4, 1976. Stark and frightening, they serve as a good introduction to his present speech.

The world food crisis has been a concern of the United States

[1] Delivered on the occasion of receiving the World Affairs Council Christian A. Herter Memorial Award, Boston, January 14, 1977. Quoted by permission.

[2] For biographical note, see Appendix.

since September 24, 1973, when Secretary of State Henry Kissinger proposed a World Food Conference in a speech before the United Nations. At the conference, held in Rome from November 5 to November 16, 1974, Kissinger said, "Our achievements, our expectations, and our moral convictions have made this into a universal political concern." (See REPRESENTATIVE AMERICAN SPEECHES: 1974-1975, p 62-96. Included in the section entitled the World Food Crisis are speeches by Earl L. Butz and Mark G. Hatfield, as well as Kissinger's address to the conference.) The only disagreement that has risen among American political leaders has been not over the worthiness of the cause but over the amount of aid to be extended because American consumers have been critical of diminishing food pools that tend to result in higher prices at the grocery stores.

Robert S. McNamara returned to the subject of world hunger when he received the annual World Affairs Council Christian A. Herter Memorial Award, at a luncheon at the Sheraton Hotel, Boston, January 14, 1977. Following the presentation by Henry Cabot Lodge, chairman of the council, the recipient spoke to an audience of over five hundred. After a typical introduction necessitated by the amenities of the occasion the president of the World Bank presented a cogent argument for world cooperation among the have-nations for "additional financial and trade support that the developed nations should supply." The speaker is most skillful in putting his statistics in a dramatic and compelling form. Into a comparatively short space he packs many specific details. The reader should note the clear, logical, and dramatic organization of the speech. (For the address to the council in 1976 by Henry A. Kissinger, see REPRESENTATIVE AMERICAN SPEECHES: 1975-1976.)

Ambassador Lodge, Ladies and Gentlemen:

I am deeply honored and grateful for this award.

Honored and grateful, because Chris Herter was—by any of half a dozen criteria—one of the great public servants of his era.

He was an immensely versatile man: diplomat, magazine publisher, Harvard lecturer, state legislator, member of Congress, governor of Massachusetts, Secretary of State.

He was a man who never allowed partisan considerations to shape his views of the proper relations between this country and the rest of the world. No one in the postwar period was a more effective proponent of bipartisan support for the broad central goals of US foreign policy.

As a Republican congressman in the Truman Administration he helped secure essential GOP approval for the Marshall Plan.

As Secretary of State in the Eisenhower Administration he mustered support in the Democratic Congress for continuity in US relationships abroad.

And in both the Kennedy and Johnson administrations —indeed, until the day he died—he served as special representative and head of delegation, in the international trade liberalization negotiations.

Chris Herter was a man whose personal warmth and unfailing courtesy were founded on a tough inner core of courage. And his civility illustrated a great truth in human affairs: that magnanimity, and compassion, and concern for others are not traits born of naiveté or weakness, but of realism and strength.

For all these reasons—and more—Governor Herter was a great credit to his state, to his country, and to the postwar world that he helped reconstruct.

It is a tradition of service that the men and women of Massachusetts know well.

Ambassador Lodge—in a pre-eminent way—personifies that tradition. His long service to the nation as legislator and diplomat, and particularly his willingness to serve not merely once, but twice, in what was at the time surely the most demanding and difficult US diplomatic post in the world—wartime Saigon—is a measure of his dedication.

Senator Brooke and other members and guests of this Council display that same sense of dedication, and that is why I am particularly grateful for this opportunity to speak to you briefly about the problems of international development.

It is, as you know, a very complex subject.

However, as I pointed out recently in Manila, there is

one central issue which more and more is affecting the thought and actions of peoples all over the globe. Equality of opportunity among men, both within nations and between nations, is becoming a major concern of our time.

It is an issue that has been gathering momentum for a century or more. The rise of the labor union movement, the drive against racial discrimination, the expansion of civil rights, the enhancement of the status of women—these and similar movements have all had an ingredient in common: the surge toward greater social justice and more equitable economic opportunity.

This broad thrust is growing more insistent today in all nations. It is searching for new solutions to the intolerable problems of poverty.

What are the dimensions of that poverty?

Let me begin with the situation of the poorest of the developing countries—those countries in which the per capita incomes are below $200. More than a billion people live in these countries. And their per capita incomes have virtually stagnated over the past decade. In statistical terms they have risen only about two dollars a year: from $130 in 1965 to $150 in 1975.

But what is beyond the power of any set of statistics to illustrate is the degradation—the inhuman degradation—the vast majority of these individuals are condemned to because of their poverty.

Malnutrition saps their energy, stunts their bodies, and shortens their lives. Illiteracy darkens their minds, and forecloses their futures. Preventable diseases maim and kill their children. Squalor and ugliness pollute and poison their surroundings.

The miraculous gift of life itself, and all its intrinsic potential—so promising and rewarding for us—is eroded and reduced for them to a desperate effort to survive.

Compared to us sitting in this room—by an accident of birth enjoying life in a developed nation—individuals in the poorest nations have:

An infant mortality rate eight times higher

A life expectancy rate one-third lower

An adult literacy rate 60 percent less

A nutritional level, for one out of every two in the population, below the minimum acceptable standards; and for millions of infants, less protein than is sufficient to permit the optimum development of the brain

The blunt fact is that poverty tends to perpetuate itself, and unless a deliberate intervention is designed and launched against its internal dynamics, it will persist and grow.

At present, the outlook for these poorest countries is appalling: over the next decade, income per capita is projected to grow at no more than 2 percent a year. For hundreds of millions of human beings that means at most an advance in income of only one or two dollars a year.

What we must understand is that unless a specific effort is made to bring these people into the development process, no feasible degree of traditional welfare, or simple redistribution of already inadequate national income, can fundamentally alter the circumstances that impoverish them.

The responsibility for such an effort lies first, of course, with the governments of the poorest countries themselves. By and large they are making that effort—on the whole far more so than most people in the developed world realize. In the past decade, the poor nations have financed over 90 percent of their development investments out of their own small incomes. But it is true that they must make even greater efforts. They have invested too little in agriculture, too little in population planning, and too little in essential public services. And too much of what they have invested has benefited only a privileged few.

Yet whatever the degree of neglect the governments in the poorest countries may have been responsible for, it has been more than matched by the failure of the international community to assist them in the development task.

The central point is that the plight of the poorest nations can only be remedied by deliberate action, and that action must be taken at both the national and international levels.

The governments of the poorest nations have to redirect their own efforts so that they will both accelerate economic growth and reduce absolute poverty. A reasonable objective for them would be to meet the basic human needs of all their peoples by the end of the century. They must begin by changing national investment priorities and by putting greater emphasis on assisting the poor to become more productive.

This will involve:

> Intensifying their efforts to expand food production
> Placing a higher priority on the expansion of exports
> Taking more determined action to moderate population growth
> And directing social services more equitably towards the poor

But although nothing can be accomplished unless these governments themselves act, they clearly cannot meet such an objective without outside assistance. Therefore the international community must help them, and help them generously.

There are four principal ways the industrial nations can make this help available:

> By additional transfers of concessional assistance
> By reallocation of some of their existing assistance
> By easing the burden of present and potential debt
> And by reducing the tariff and non-tariff barriers that continue to discriminate against many of the exports of the poorest countries

In particular, if poverty is to be reduced, then developed nations must squarely face the fact that current and projected levels of Official Development Assistance (ODA) for the poorest countries are disgracefully inadequate.

In 1975, ODA amounted to about .36 percent of the GNP of the industrialized nations—one half of the target set by the General Assembly five years before. Moreover, on the basis of present plans, not only is there no hope that the target can ever be reached, but there is a serious possibility that performance over the remaining years of the decade may erode even further.

It may be of interest to the members of this Council that the United States—the country with the largest GNP in the world—is currently one of the poorest performers in the matter of Official Development Assistance. Among the developed nations, Sweden, the Netherlands, Norway, Australia, France, Belgium, Denmark, Canada, New Zealand, Germany and even—with all its economic problems—the United Kingdom: all of these nations devote a greater percentage of their GNP to Official Development Assistance than does the United States.

In 1949, at the beginning of the Marshall Plan—the Marshall Plan for which Chris Herter as a Republican congressman in a Democratic Administration worked so hard —US Official Development Assistance amounted to 2.79 percent of GNP. Today, it is one tenth of that: .27 percent of GNP. And this after a quarter-century of real growth in personal incomes in the United States, which has more than doubled the standard of life for the average American in any terms in which you want to measure it: salaries, ownership of homes, automobiles, second television sets, beef consumption, leisure-time activities; almost any category you can name.

Even dogs and cats in America today have a better standard of nutrition than tens of millions of children in the developing nations. But US Official Development Assistance to those nations has not only not kept pace with its own growing domestic affluence. It has very substantially declined.

The economies of the developed nations—already immensely productive—will become even more productive over the next few years. For them to increase their help to the poorest countries would not require them to diminish in the slightest their own high standards of living, but only to devote a tiny percentage of the additional per capita real income they will earn over the decade.

If the governments of the poorest countries do not take the internal measures they must, and if the developed nations do not help them with the development assistance they so seriously need, then the outlook for three out of every four of the more than one billion human beings who live in these disadvantaged countries is unspeakably grim.

These, then, are the elements of a program to accelerate economic growth and to reduce absolute poverty in the poorest nations. What is the situation in the developing countries with per capita incomes over $200 per year—the so-called middle-income developing countries—the Brazils, Mexicos, Turkeys, and Koreas?

The outlook for them is much more favorable. As a group, they have achieved an overall growth rate during the past decade of almost 7 percent—about 4 percent in per capita terms.

As compared with the poorest nations, they have been able to take advantage of their more favorable endowment in resources, better market opportunities, and increased capital flows.

Their 900 million citizens now enjoy an average per capita income about 50 percent higher than ten years ago. On the whole, it is fair to say that the middle-income developing nations have begun to establish a promising structure for high economic growth rates.

They face, however, two serious problems.

The momentum of their growth has been sharply interrupted since 1973. On a per capita basis, it fell to 1.5 percent last year as a direct consequence of the recession in their export markets, the increase in their energy costs, the deterioration in their terms of trade, and the persistent worldwide inflation.

And equally disturbing is the fact that in many of these countries there has been a serious neglect of equity in the distribution of employment opportunities, and in the allocation of public services that affect productivity. The inevitable result has been a severely skewed pattern of income distribution.

They have increased their gross national products over the decade, but the benefits of this growth have accrued disproportionately to the already more favored upper-income groups in their societies, and broadened rather than narrowed the gap between the privileged and the deprived.

Though these countries do enjoy some distinct advantages over the poorest nations, the fact remains that collectively they, too, contain large numbers of individuals—some 170 million—trapped in absolute poverty.

There are hundreds of millions more in what I have termed "relative poverty"; that is, persons with incomes somewhat above the absolute poverty level, but less than one third of the national average. These individuals may feel even more frustrated than those in the poorest nations, since they live in an environment of visible economic growth. Their societies are progressing rapidly, but they are not.

The governments of these nations must recognize the necessity of assuring broader participation of their peoples in the process of development. That means assisting the poor to become more productive at the same time as steps are taken to increase the mobilization of internal resources, to broaden the range of export products, and to expand the coverage of export markets in order to accelerate national growth rates.

In turn, the developed nations must find practical ways to assist these developing countries by allowing them more equitable access to markets, and by making available additional development capital on reasonable terms.

Although the formula for economic advance in the middle-income countries differs from that applicable to the poorest nations, the action required is similar in one important respect: both groups of nations need additional support from the developed world if they are to achieve acceptable rates of growth.

It is the recognition of this fact which led a year ago last September to the Seventh Special Session of the General Assembly; to the meeting of UNCTAD in Nairobi last spring; and to the North-South Dialogue which continues in Paris.

And yet, to date, after more than a year of intense debate, there has been no agreement on the level of additional assistance to be provided to the developing nations.

The reason for the lack of agreement is, I think, obvious: the discussions have focused far too much on details rather than on fundamentals.

What is needed is a basic understanding among the parties as to:

> The nature and magnitude of the problem
> The action required to address it
> The relative responsibilities of the parties for taking such action
> The costs and benefits to each of doing so

Once the broad limits of such a meeting of minds have been established—a global compact, if you will—then the specific form of assistance to be provided by individual developed nations to particular developing countries could be examined. It would then become apparent very quickly that it is relatively unimportant whether the assistance is to take the form of commodity agreements, debt relief, trade concessions, bilateral aid, or multilateral financing—or any particular combination of these—provided the overall total is adequate.

In view of the continuing impasse at official levels, it seems to me that the chances of reaching such an understanding might be improved if a high-level, but deliberately unofficial, commission were organized to analyze the problem, and to recommend action to be taken by both developed and developing nations.

Such a private commission should clearly be drawn from individuals—from both the rich and poor nations—who have either had practical political experience in dealing with development issues, or who have demonstrated outstanding professional competence in development economics.

The chairman and convener of such a commission ought to be a person of the great political experience and stature, say, of a Willy Brandt, the former chancellor of the Federal Republic of Germany.

The chairman and members of the commission would have the advantage of collaborating not as official representatives of particular countries, or blocs of nations, but rather as international figures of recognized competence and independent judgment, whose mandate it would be to formulate those basic proposals on which global agreement is both essential and possible.

The funding required for the commission's work would be modest, and to ensure the commission's independence the cost could be shared by a number of governments, international institutions, and private foundations. I have already received indications from Minister Pronk of the Netherlands, and Mr. David Hopper, president of Canada's International Development Research Center, that they would be willing to consider participating in such financing.

Such a commission cannot be expected, of course, to provide an instant, comprehensive, all-purpose solution to the problems of development—for none exists.

But what one could realistically expect from such a private, high-level independent group is the careful identification of those political decisions which can command public and legislative support in rich and poor countries alike, and hence enable the international community to break out of the current impasse.

There will be some critics who say that it is fanciful to suppose that the rich and poor nations—all of them politically sensitive over their own national prerogatives—can come to any meaningful understanding over development issues.

I do not believe that is true.

What I do believe is that such an understanding is unlikely to come about in the current international climate of contentious debate.

And I want to stress again that what is essential is to determine the overall volume of additional financial and trade support that the developed nations should supply; the additional policy reforms and structural changes the developing nations should undertake; and how these two mutual efforts can be more effectively applied to meeting the needs of the two billion people in the developing world.

It would be the commission's role to help make that happen.

It is true that the world today is divided on a whole spectrum of issues: political, economic, ideological, cultural.

It would be naive to pretend otherwise.

But surely there is one issue on which none of us can disagree.

And that is that a greater degree of equity must be achieved both within nations and among nations.

The commission's task, the international community's task—indeed, the task of all of us here in this room—is to help move that forward.

MEETING WORLD FOOD NEEDS [3]

JOHN A. HANNAH [4]

The preceding speech, by Robert S. McNamara, president of the World Bank, constitutes an excellent introduction to this speech by John A. Hannah, executive director of the World Food Council, delivered to the annual meeting of the American Farm Bureau Federation in Honolulu, January 10, 1977. The conference had been arranged to discuss the world food situation as it affects US agriculture. Sixteen thousand farm and ranch members were present for the convention.

Dr. Hannah has been active on the issues of world development since his involvement in 1949 in the US Point Four Program of technical assistance to developing countries. For a number of years he served as administrator of the US Agency for International Development. He was one of the chief planners of the 1974 World Food Conference in Rome and was appointed the first executive director of the World Food Council on January 15, 1975, by the secretary-general of the United Nations. He speaks from great knowledge and with great concern for the world's food needs.

The McNamara address and the Hannah address provide a study in contrast—in adjusting similar material to a very different audience. In speaking on "the problem of international development" to the World Affairs Council, a cosmopolitan organization, McNamara gave a broad view of what is needed and attempted to create sympathy for "a billion people" condemned to "squalor and ugliness" that pollutes and poisons "their surroundings." He worked primarily to stir sympathy and compassion. But Hannah perhaps had a more difficult task—he had to bring into balance selfishness and altruism. He tempered his motive appeals to farmers' material gains with a plea for understanding, fair play, and compassion. He suggested that solving world hunger promotes security to American farmers—that is, he stressed how the American farmer's security is closely tied to his willingness to help feed the hungry abroad. Side by side he included personally oriented and socially oriented appeals. He made his point when he said:

[3] Delivered at the annual meeting of the American Farm Bureau Federation at Sheraton-Waikiki Hotel, Honolulu, January 10, 1977. Quoted by permission.
[4] For biographical note, see Appendix.

It is most important that we realize that, more important than percentages of population increases or quantities of food available to feed them, is the fact that we are talking about *poor, hungry, hopeful people*. Hundreds of millions of men, women and children whose futures, whose perspectives on life, whose values and whose capacities to appreciate being alive depend largely on the willingness and ability now of the countries of the world to take up the challenge of helping food-deficit countries to provide themselves with an adequate supply of food.

Mr. Chairman, Fellow Members of the American Farm Bureau Federation and their guests, Ladies and Gentlemen,

I am happy to be here. The letter of invitation from President Allan Grant suggested that I discuss "The world food situation from the standpoint of world food needs in the next decade and US agriculture's challenges to produce these food needs at a profit to US farmers."

Let me speak first to the question of "profit" to US farmers. The world's food needs in the years ahead can only be met by the efforts of farmers all over the world. These farmers, whether subsisting on less than an acre in South Asia or Africa or elsewhere, or on a large modern farm in the United States, cannot be expected to meet this challenge unless they receive adequate rewards and incentives. There can be no question about that. Therefore what I have to say to you today is with the full understanding that the food challenge must be met *at a profit* to farmers. And by profit I mean an adequate return to the farmer for his costs—his land, his investments, his implements—and a fair return for his labor, his worry and his risks. Farmers all around the world cannot be expected to produce their maximum production unless there is a market for the food produced that covers all the costs. The improved seeds and the fertilizers and pesticides and other costs of production will not be assumed by American farmers or farmers on the little farms of Asia, Africa or Latin America without some assurance that the selling price will more than cover all normal production costs.

The food needs of the next decade are not simply a challenge to American farmers, or to US agriculture, or to the United States. They are a challenge to all farmers, especially the small farmers in poor countries where people are hungry and not enough food is produced. Meeting these food needs is a challenge not only to food producers but to governments and consumers everywhere. The food problem is a worldwide problem and must be solved at the world level. We are all involved whether we want to be or not.

To my mind, *the* greatest challenge of this last quarter of the twentieth century is the challenge the world faces of providing food for the world's hungry people in the years ahead.

It is a challenge for you, the farmers of America, who are experts in the production of food. It is a challenge to the farmers and consumers of food all over the world.

It is not simply the challenge of producing more food, but also the challenge of understanding *what the food problem of the world is* and *where* and *how it must be solved.*

The world food problem has been a source of international concern repeatedly in the past quarter-century and long before that, but the challenge was not taken very seriously as a problem of concern to the whole world until the United Nations World Food Conference in Rome in November 1974, twenty-six months ago.

What is the challenge?

First, let me restate it. The challenge is how is the world to feed its *hungry* people in the years immediately ahead. It is embodied in the Declaration on the Eradication of Hunger and Malnutrition in these words:

Every man, woman and child has the inalienable right to be free from hunger and malnutrition in order to develop fully and maintain their physical and mental faculties. Society today already possesses sufficient resources, organizational ability, and technology and hence the competence to achieve this objective.

This declaration was adopted by the World Food Conference and endorsed by the General Assembly of the United Nations following the World Food Conference in December 1974.

This challenge, even its formulation, was critically influenced by the statement of the Secretary of State of the United States at the World Food Conference when he said:

The profound promise of our era is that for the first time we may have the technical capacity to free mankind from the scourge of hunger. Therefore, today we must proclaim a bold objective—that within a decade no child will go to bed hungry, that no family will fear for its next day's bread, and that no human being's future and capacities will be stunted by malnutrition.

I emphasize this formulation because it is important to recognize that the issue is not simply one of producing more food *for people in general.* The world has done this consistently in the past—populations have increased rapidly and life spans have been extended—and will undoubtedly continue to do so in the future. The more than 4 billion people alive today have more food available than the 2.5 billion people alive in 1950 had—about one fifth more per person. But this in *on the average!* Underneath this *average* is the real food problem and the real challenge we face today—those tens of millions of starving, hungry or grossly malnourished people—most of them children.

Over the past quarter-century a growing imbalance in food production and consumption has emerged in the world. The developed countries—of which the United States is one of the most developed and by far the most significant producer and exporter of food in the world—have mastered the techniques and policies appropriate to producing not only *enough* food but more than enough. They have been able to do this in part because they are developed, which means their people have the educations and incomes appropriate to a high level of food consumption and production. This capacity to produce more than enough food gave rise to two important phenomena that characterized the food world from the end of World War II until 1972 with:

First, the accumulation of large stocks of cereal grains in North America which protected the world against unexpected calamities; and

Second, the generous provision by North America (Canada and the United States) of food aid for emergencies and for poor countries whose food supplies were inadequate and who were unable to import commercially the large amounts of food required to feed their hungry people.

But in the developing countries, less desirable phenomena were emerging. During the decade of the 1950s food production in the developing countries was growing about as rapidly as in the developed countries and more rapidly than population. In the decade of the 1960s however, the developing countries experienced both more rapid population growth and a slowing down in their rate of increase in their own food production. By the middle of the 1960s food production in the developing countries was no longer keeping up with population growth. During the first five years of the decade of the 1970s, it slipped even more seriously. As a result, the developing countries—into which are born about 85 percent of all the children born on this earth —were no longer able to feed themselves let alone improve the level of nutrition for their malnourished people.

These developments have had two important and sobering consequences. The developing countries, which were virtually self-sufficient in their food supplies in 1950 were importing annually between 25 and 30 million tons of grain in the late 1960s, half of which was in the form of food aid, and by 1975 the gross imports of these countries had reached more than 50 million tons per year. The World Food Conference projections of the food situation for 1985 and beyond predicted a doubling of these cereals imports to a required total—from 85 to 100 million tons or more per year—unless there is a fundamental improvement in the capacity to produce food *in* the food-deficit developing countries.

In recent years, each year additional developing countries have ceased being self-sufficient in food production and the total food import requirements of those already in food deficit has increased. The first challenge is to increase food production in the developing countries.

The second and more complex, but even more important, challenge is to see to it that the increased food supplies are actually consumed by those people who need additional food most. At the time of the World Food Conference in November 1974, 460 million people were estimated to suffer from serious malnutrition—460 million people—that is almost twice the population of the United States. Critics may quibble about whether the figures should be 400 million or 500 million, but the fact that there is extensive hunger and malnutrition in the world is not in question. Most of the malnourished people live in Asia, another large fraction of them live in Africa, and there are large groups of malnourished people in some Latin American countries and elsewhere in the world. These people live mostly in rural areas, although malnutrition is evident to any observant visitor in most of the larger cities in most of the world's developing countries. And the least well nourished are the women and children—the future citizens of this world and those who will be most instrumental in teaching them about the world.

If the challenge to eradicate serious hunger and malnutrition in a decade is to be seriously faced—and you and I know in our hearts that it should be—we must attack the problem where it is and this is not simply a matter of increasing food production.

The third challenge is the development of a new, realistic and adequate system of food security, which inevitably means a system of food stocks.

Food is the most necessary of all human needs, especially the basic cereals, rice, wheat and the other food grains and the oil seeds that are the principal diet for poor people in the poorest countries.

When there is a little bit too much food, prices are low and farmers have little incentive to expand production. When there is not quite enough food to go around, prices can reach incredibly high levels and hungry, poor people get hungrier and poorer, and that is particularly true in the least developed countries lacking foreign exchange to pay for food.

The basic uncertainties that surround farming, especially cereals production, require some system of food reserves that ensures equitable prices to farmers and consumers and assures that production will be stimulated when and where it is needed.

For four years the world has balanced precariously on the thin edge of each year's food supply. At first this produced high prices for many farmers and hardships for many of the world's poorest consumers. Now it is producing declines in farm prices, but consumers prices are not falling proportionally and many farm-input prices have remained high.

In the past two years, efforts to formulate an effective world policy to build and manage a grain reserve that makes sense have gotten nowhere. No serious-minded person would advocate a return to the unplanned and un-thought-thru accumulation and use of grain stocks in North America that typified the fifties and sixties. Now is the time to give serious thought to the establishment of food reserves or buffer stocks (if you prefer these words) that will truly benefit both producers and consumers. The United States should play a leading role in encouraging serious discussions of all the pros and cons.

It is generally recognized that the pattern of world food production, food aid and food surpluses that prevailed during the past two decades was unsatisfactory. It produced the progressively deteriorating conditions that came to light with such force during the world food crisis of 1972-1974. These patterns of production and consumption and the policies which underlie them should not be returned to.

The inadequate levels of food production in the food-deficit developing countries cannot be reversed by those countries alone without outside encouragement. Additional external resources, both capital and technical assistance, must be provided by those countries in a position to do so.

There is a useful role for food aid. Not careless food aid. Not food aid as a by-product of surplus disposal programmes. But food aid with a real intent and purpose: designed to help feed hungry people; to support efforts in developing countries to increase their own food production or to advance other development efforts that will provide the increased foreign-exchange income necessary to buy more food; and to assist in the transition from negative to positive food production policies.

A responsible attitude toward world food security must include some kind of coherent and adequate system of food reserves, especially grain stocks.

After two decades of trying to cope with the burden of surplus grain stocks which taxpayers had to pay for and farmers disliked because of the depressed grain prices, it is understandable that in the developed, grain exporting countries there is a degree of relief that these surpluses are gone. But for the world as a whole this is a very dangerous situation.

All of this is part of the challenge as I see it. It is a challenge with three major facets:

One, to increase the food production capacity of the poor, food-deficit countries where gross malnutrition is most serious;

Two, to raise the level of nutrition of the world's poor and hungry and too often starving people; and

Three, to make the world secure against those calamities of nature and man which cannot be predicted but which we all know will occur from time to time.

One of the real needs in today's world is the development by all enlightened nations of National Food Policies arrived at after full understanding and discussion at all levels of the problems of the food producers (the farmers), of the food requirements of all people (the consumers), and of the role of governments at all levels.

The United States does not have now and never has had a national food policy. When we have reached policy decisions they have been reached in periods of stress to deal with farm prices or farm surpluses or as a result of political motivation. The American Farm Bureau Federation could play a very useful role if it should decide to urge a full national discussion of this whole matter—to be arrived at over time with all of the cards from all interested groups on the table.

If we had a thought-through and agreed-upon and understood United States Food Policy, the US would be in a much better position to play a useful and constructive role in the development of long-range plans and for participation by the US in dealing with world food problems.

Why is it important to solve these problems?

It is difficult for many American farmers to see, or to feel intensely, just how these food problems relate to them. But I assure you they do. They are profoundly relevant to you and they will continue to be important and immediate elements in the daily lives of your children and grandchildren, and of mine, for a long time ahead.

The more than 4 billion people now on this earth will have increased to about 6-1/4 billion at the end of this century, twenty-three years from now. The food deficits of the developing countries now projected for the decade beginning in 1985 are too high to be considered manageable but are only a fraction of those that can be projected for the long years ahead unless immediate and adequate steps are taken to change the pattern of the last two decades.

It is most important that we realize that, more important than percentages of population increases or quantities of food available to feed them, is the fact that we are talking about *poor, hungry, hopeful* people. Hundreds of millions of men, women and children whose futures, whose perspectives on life, whose values and whose capacities to appreciate being alive depend largely on the willingness and ability now of the countries of the world to take up the challenge of helping food-deficit countries to provide themselves with an adequate supply of food. If the people of our countries are unwilling to take up this challenge now with deeds and actions that actually help to bring about change, we will not have adequately provided for our own children's future.

The World Food Conference called for the establishment of institutions to ensure that the people of the world will face up to this problem.

I hope you will pardon me for speaking of the two which I have been especially close to and for which I have great personal hope.

The World Food Conference, in its Resolution XIII, called for the establishment of an International Fund for Agricultural Development if sufficient additional resources could be generated to support such a fund.

The secretary-general of the United Nations assigned to me the responsibility of determining whether such funds could be generated and to organize the intergovernmental discussions necessary to bring such a fund into being. It is a matter of great personal satisfaction for me to be able to remind you that in less than two years this fund, which started as only an idea, has become a reality. It was possible for Kurt Waldheim, secretary-general of the United Nations, to announce on December 20 that the goal target of $1,000 million pledged by the governments of the world had been exceeded and that the Articles of Agreement for IFAD which had been worked out and agreed upon and initialled by ninety-one countries were declared open for signature.

The first country to sign the agreement was the United States. All of the members of the OECD (the countries of Western Europe, Japan, Australia and New Zealand, Canada and the United States) are contributing with a total of $567 million, all twelve of the OPEC countries are contributing with a total of $435.5 million and the developing recipient countries have pledged about $20 million, bringing the overall total of the fund to $1,022 million.

The Fund is a unique institution. Its underlying financial support is new. Its voting structure is also new, divided equally among the developed countries, the OPEC countries and the developing potential recipient countries. The developing countries will have a substantial role in determining the policies and activities of the Fund.

The fund will be managed as a business contracting with the World Bank and the Regional Banks, and other international organizations or national agencies or private corporations to carry on the business of determining the criteria to qualify for loans to be used only for projects and programs that will actually increase food production.

The management will have all the potential of any corporate entity with final executive authority in the hands of an elected executive board and president. The first one billion dollars is planned to be loaned over the first three years after which the fund will come back to the donor countries for a replenishment. It is designed to provide a new source of concessional loans at a level of about $350 million per year.

The first priority in the fund's activities will be the stimulation of food production in the poorest developing countries with first emphasis on the food-deficit countries. The creation of this fund is a clear indication that the countries of the world are ready to provide the resources necessary to seriously begin to solve the world food problem and at the same time are willing to do so with a new type of institution which will help to bridge the gap that has so often separated the rich and the poor. Of all the many initiatives launched in recent years to get the developed countries and the OPEC countries to work cooperatively together toward solving the world's serious problems the only one that has actually succeeded is IFAD. It is hoped that through it both groups will learn how to join in doing what is clearly in the interest of both groups and, more important, good for all the world.

The World Food Council is another product of the World Food Conference. It was created to give guidance and direction to international efforts to solve the world food problem. Its role is to monitor the policies and programs of the international agencies dealing with food and those of governments to ensure that the major food problems are tackled and that the necessary resources and political support are generated to solve them.

The World Food Council consists of thirty-six member governments and a secretariat of about a dozen professional people, with supporting staff, of which I am proud to be the executive director. Representation in the council is also unique. Almost two thirds of its members are developing or OPEC countries. The rest are developed countries and Socialist countries. The United States is a member of the council and so is the Soviet Union. This is an important fact since participation by the USSR in international organizations dealing with food has been minimal. The present membership consists of nine African countries, eight from Asia, seven from Latin America, four from the Socialist countries of Eastern Europe and eight members from Western Europe and other developed countries. They are: Argentina, Australia, Bangladesh, Canada, Chad, Cuba, Egypt, France, Federal Republic of Germany, Guatemala, Hungary, Indonesia, Iran, Italy, Ivory Coast, Jamaica, Japan, Kenya, Madagascar, Mauritania, Mexico, Nigeria, Pakistan, Philippines, Poland, Rwanda, Somalia, Sri Lanka, Sweden, Thailand, Trinidad and Tobago, USSR, United Kingdom, United States, Venezuela and Yugoslavia. Each member country is represented in the council by a minister of that country.

The World Food Council has a long way to go to live up to the responsibilities assigned to it. As a new international body it has had to face the problem of how to work together to solve specific problems when these problems are often the result of very real political differences between countries. It is the first body in the United Nations system made up of ministers of government.

The council is making progress. It has on its plate some of the serious issues which must be faced if the world food problems are to be solved: increased food production in the food-deficit developing countries, improved food aid and dealing with the complicated problems of world food security.

Ladies and gentlemen, these are only beginning steps but they are in the right direction. Repeatedly in the past the world food problem has been dramatically presented and then quietly allowed to drift from the minds of those who were concerned. The World Food Council was established to ensure that this does not happen again, and that the world's attention will be constantly focused on the need to make fundamental improvements and that ways to accomplish the desired objectives will be brought to the attention of international agencies and national governments. The dimensions of the world food problem are known—where it is, who suffers the most and, within limits, why it is. We think we now know how to move in directions that will produce results.

At the outset of this statement, I purposely noted that both the Declaration on the Eradication of Hunger and Malnutrition and Secretary of State Kissinger's statement made it clear that the world has the resources and the technical capabilities for solving the world food problem and for making certain that "within a decade no child will go to bed hungry and that no family will fear for its next day's bread, and that no human being's future and capacities will be stunted by malnutrition."

The problem is not simple—and the solution will not be easily achieved.

It is our hope that the World Food Council can and will

serve as a vital link between those who possess the resources and the techniques and those who are only poor, hungry and hopeful.

It is my hope that the agricultural leadership of the United States will not limit their role to the production of food and fiber but will expand their interests in stimulating an adequate understanding on the part of all Americans of the complexity and the importance of progress toward constructive solutions to the problems of feeding the world's hungry people.

I am confident that this time the world will recognize that what it knows it should do, it can do—and will do.

CHOICES FOR THE FUTURE

ENERGY PROBLEMS [1]

JIMMY CARTER [2]

The 1973-1974 oil embargo and the fuel shortage during the winter of 1976-1977 dramatically demonstrated that the United States has an energy problem. Oil imports constitute 40 percent of what is now used. Consumption increases year by year. Drivers are buying big, "gas-guzzling" cars at an increasing rate. Predictions are that fossil fuel may soon be exhausted. But recent polls indicate these dramatic developments seem to have made little impression on 50 percent of the American people who seem to think that the shortages are contrived by big oil companies, that vast new discoveries are about to take place, that new technology is sure to save us.

An editorial in the New York *Times* (April 24, 1977) summarized the situation as follows:

> Americans are energy alcoholics. For half a century, we have reveled in cheap oil, gas and electricity. Not content with one car, we have bought two and three. Not content with toasters, we have generated a whole sub-industry to tantalize us with electric carving knives, crepe pans, cookie shooters. Natural gas is a premium home-heating fuel in limited supply; we use it to heat commercial boilers that could readily employ coal instead. But energy is worth more than Americans pay for it—and is rapidly becoming dearer still. If the revel continues, the morning after will be long and painful indeed.

Remembering Harry Truman's statement that "the buck stops here," President Carter has taken a firm stand on what needs to be done about energy. On April 18 at 8:00 P.M. (EST) speaking from the Oval Office in the White House, he took the issue to the people via television. He looked directly into the lens of the television camera, giving the appearance of extemporaneous delivery. But actually he used a teleprompter attached to the camera (New York *Times*, April 19, 1977). His evening appearance

[1] Delivered via television and radio from the Oval Office of the White House, Washington, D.C., on April 18, 1977, at 8:00 P.M. (EST). From *Weekly Compilation of Presidential Documents*, vol. 13, no. 17, p 560-5.

[2] For biographical note, see Appendix.

was reminiscent of the Fireside Chats which became a regular practice during Franklin D. Roosevelt's four terms. Carter has sought to establish a similar rapport with the voters.

The April 18 talk marked a change in the President's mood and manner. He was "deliberately sober," saying in his opening sentence that he was going to give "an unpleasant talk about a problem unprecedented in our history. With the exception of preventing war, this is the greatest challenge our country will face during our lifetime." James Reston (New York *Times,* April 24, 1977) thought that there was impact in "the philosophy" that the President presented. Reston stated Carter was "simply saying that we are running out of gas and getting in a jam, and that this is not a regional, political, or a class problem. He is asking us to do hard things with our minds: to think about shortages in a time of plenty, and to imagine the lives of our children, and even of the entire human family, at the end of the century." One reporter described the speech as "calm and clinical, short on rhetoric, bereft of smiles" (Mary McGrory of the Washington *Star*). The *Christian Science Monitor* (April 22, 1977) called it a "courageous and historic call for a concerted battle against energy waste." This broadcast was Carter's most important speech to that time in his Administration.

Good evening:

Tonight I want to have an unpleasant talk with you about a problem that is unprecedented in our history. With the exception of preventing war, this is the greatest challenge that our country will face during our lifetime.

The energy crisis has not yet overwhelmed us, but it will if we do not act quickly. It's a problem that we will not be able to solve in the next few years, and it's likely to get progressively worse through the rest of this century.

We must not be selfish or timid if we hope to have a decent world for our children and our grandchildren. We simply must balance our demand for energy with our rapidly shrinking resources. By acting now we can control our future instead of letting the future control us.

Two days from now, I will present to the Congress my energy proposals. Its members will be my partners, and they have already given me a great deal of valuable advice.

Many of these proposals will be unpopular. Some will

cause you to put up with inconveniences and to make sacrifices. The most important thing about these proposals is that the alternative may be a national catastrophe. Further delay can affect our strength and our power as a nation.

Our decision about energy will test the character of the American people and the ability of the President and the Congress to govern this nation. This difficult effort will be the moral equivalent of war, except that we will be uniting our efforts to build and not to destroy.

Now, I know that some of you may doubt that we face real energy shortages. The 1973 gas lines are gone and with this springtime weather, our homes are warm again. But our energy problem is worse tonight than it was in 1973 or a few weeks ago in the dead of winter. It's worse because more waste has occurred and more time has passed by without our planning for the future. And it will get worse every day until we act.

The oil and natural gas that we rely on for 75 percent of our energy are simply running out. In spite of increased effort, domestic production has been dropping steadily at about 6 percent a year. Imports have doubled in the last five years. Our nation's economic and political independence is becoming increasingly vulnerable. Unless profound changes are made to lower oil consumption, we now believe that early in the 1980s the world will be demanding more oil that it can produce.

The world now uses about 60 million barrels of oil a day, and demand increases each year about 5 percent. This means that just to stay even we need the production of a new Texas every year, an Alaskan North Slope every nine months, or a new Saudi Arabia every three years. Obviously, this cannot continue.

We must look back into history to understand our energy problem. Twice in the last several hundred years, there has been a transition in the way people use energy.

The first was about two hundred years ago, when we changed away from wood—which had provided about 90 percent of all fuel—to coal, which was much more efficient. This change became the basis of the Industrial Revolution.

The second change took place in this century, with the growing use of oil and natural gas. They were more convenient and cheaper than coal, and the supply seemed to be almost without limit. They made possible the age of automobile and airplane travel. Nearly everyone who is alive today grew up during this period, and we have never known anything different.

Because we are now running out of gas and oil, we must prepare quickly for a third change—to strict conservation and to the renewed use of coal and to permanent renewable energy sources like solar power.

The world has not prepared for the future. During the 1950s, people used twice as much oil as during the 1940s. During the 1960s, we used twice as much as during the 1950s. And in each of those decades, more oil was consumed than in all of man's previous history combined.

World consumption of oil is still going up. If it were possible to keep it rising during the 1970s and 1980s by 5 percent a year as it has in the past, we could use up all the proven reserves of oil in the entire world by the end of the next decade.

I know that many of you have suspected that some supplies of oil and gas are being withheld from the market. You may be right, but suspicions about the oil companies cannot change the fact that we are running out of petroleum.

All of us have heard about the large oil fields on Alaska's North Slope. In a few years, when the North Slope is producing fully, its total output will be just about equal to 2 years' increase in our own nation's energy demand.

Each new inventory of world oil reserves has been more disturbing than the last. World oil production can probably keep going up for another six or eight years. But sometime in the 1980s, it can't go up any more. Demand will overtake production. We have no choice about that.

But we do have a choice about how we will spend the next few years. Each American uses the energy equivalent of sixty barrels of oil per person each year. Ours is the most wasteful nation on earth. We waste more energy than we import. With about the same standard of living, we use twice as much energy per person as do other countries like Germany, Japan, and Sweden.

One choice, of course, is to continue doing what we've been doing before. We can drift along for a few more years. Our consumption of oil would keep going up every year. Our cars would continue to be too large and inefficient. Three quarters of them would carry only one person —the driver—while our public transportation system continues to decline. We can delay insulating our homes, and they will continue to lose about 50 percent of their heat in waste. We can continue using scarce oil and natural gas to generate electricity and continue wasting two thirds of their fuel value in the process.

If we do not act, then by 1985 we will be using 33 percent more energy than we use today.

We can't substantially increase our domestic production, so we would need to import twice as much oil as we do now. Supplies will be uncertain. The cost will keep going up. Six years ago, we paid $3.7 billion for imported oil. Last year we spent $36 billion for imported oil—nearly 10 times as much—and this year we may spend $45 billion.

Unless we act, we will spend more than $550 billion for imported oil by 1985—more than $2,500 for every man, woman, and child in America. Along with that money that we transport overseas, we will continue losing American jobs and become increasingly vulnerable to supply interruptions.

Now we have a choice. But if we wait, we will constantly live in fear of embargoes. We could endanger our freedom as a sovereign nation to act in foreign affairs. Within ten years, we would not be able to import enough oil from any country, at any acceptable price.

If we wait and do not act, then our factories will not be able to keep our people on the job with reduced supplies of fuel.

Too few of our utility companies will have switched to coal, which is our most abundant energy source. We will not be ready to keep our transportation system running with smaller and more efficient cars and a better network of buses, trains, and public transportation.

We will feel mounting pressure to plunder the environment. We will have to have a crash program to build more nuclear plants, strip mine and burn more coal, and drill more offshore wells than if we begin to conserve right now.

Inflation will soar; production will go down; people will lose their jobs. Intense competition for oil will build up among nations and also among the different regions within our own country. This has already started.

If we fail to act soon, we will face an economic, social, and political crisis that will threaten our free institutions. But we still have another choice. We can begin to prepare right now. We can decide to act while there is still time. That is the concept of the energy policy that we will present on Wednesday.

Our national energy plan is based on ten fundamental principles. The first principle is that we can have an effective and comprehensive energy policy only if the government takes responsibility for it and if the people understand the seriousness of the challenge and are willing to make sacrifices.

The second principle is that healthy economic growth must continue. Only by saving energy can we maintain our standard of living and keep our people at work. An effective conservation program will create hundreds of thousands of new jobs.

The third principle is that we must protect the environment. Our energy problems have the same cause as our environmental problems—wasteful use of resources. Conservation helps us solve both problems at once.

The fourth principle is that we must reduce our vulnerability to potentially devastating embargoes. We can protect ourselves from uncertain supplies by reducing our demand for oil, by making the most of our abundant resources such as coal, and by developing a strategic petroleum reserve.

The fifth principle is that we must be fair. Our solutions must ask equal sacrifices from every region, every class of people, and every interest group. Industry will have to do its part to conserve just as consumers will. The energy producers deserve fair treatment, but we will not let the oil companies profiteer.

The sixth principle, and the cornerstone of our policy, is to reduce demand through conservation. Our emphasis on conservation is a clear difference between this plan and others which merely encouraged crash production efforts. Conservation is the quickest, cheapest, most practical source of energy. Conservation is the only way that we can buy a barrel of oil for about $2. It costs about $13 to waste it.

The seventh principle is that prices should generally reflect the true replacement cost of energy. We are only cheating ourselves if we make energy artificially cheap and use more than we can really afford.

The eighth principle is that government policies must be predictable and certain. Both consumers and producers need policies they can count on so they can plan ahead. This is one reason that I'm working with the Congress to create a new Department of Energy to replace more than fifty different agencies that now have some control over energy.

The ninth principle is that we must conserve the fuels that are scarcest and make the most of those that are plentiful. We can't continue to use oil and gas for 75 percent of our consumption, as we do now, when they only make up 7 percent of our domestic reserves. We need to shift to plentiful coal, while taking care to protect the environment, and to supply stricter safety standards to nuclear energy.

The tenth and last principle is that we must start now to develop the new, unconventional sources of energy that we will rely on in the next century.

Now, these ten principles have guided the development of the policy that I will describe to you and the Congress on Wednesday night.

Our energy plan will also include a number of specific goals to measure our progress toward a stable energy system. These are the goals that we set for 1985:

☐ to reduce the annual growth rate in our energy demand to less than 2 percent

☐ to reduce gasoline consumption by 10 percent below its current level

☐ to cut in half the portion of US oil which is imported—from a potential level of 16 million barrels to 6 million barrels a day

☐ to establish a strategic petroleum reserve of one billion barrels, more than a six-months supply

☐ to increase our coal production by about two thirds to more than one billion tons a year

☐ to insulate 90 percent of American homes and all new buildings

☐ to use solar energy in more than 2½ million houses

We will monitor our progress toward these goals year-by-year. Our plan will call for strict conservation measures if we fall behind. I can't tell you that these measures will be easy, nor will they be popular. But I think most of you realize that a policy which does not ask for changes or sacrifices would not be an effective policy at this late date.

This plan is essential to protect our jobs, our environment, our standard of living, and our future. Whether this plan truly makes a difference will not be decided now here in Washington but in every town and every factory, in every home and on every highway and every farm.

I believe that this can be a positive challenge. There is something especially American in the kind of changes that we have to make. We've always been proud, through our history, of being efficient people. We've always been proud of our ingenuity, our skill at answering questions. Now we need efficiency and ingenuity more than ever.

We've always been proud of our leadership in the world. And now we have a chance again to give the world a positive example.

We've always been proud of our vision of the future. We've always wanted to give our children and our grandchildren a world richer in possibilities than we have had ourselves. They are the ones that we must provide for now. They are the ones who will suffer most if we don't act.

I've given you some of the principles of the plan. I'm sure that each of you will find something you don't like about the specifics of our proposal. It will demand that we make sacrifices and changes in every life. To some degree, the sacrifices will be painful—but so is any meaningful sacrifice. It will lead to some higher costs and to some greater inconvenience for everyone. But the sacrifices can be gradual, realistic, and they are necessary. Above all, they will be fair. No one will gain an unfair advantage through this plan. No one will be asked to bear an unfair burden.

We will monitor the accuracy of data from the oil and natural gas companies for the first time, so that we will always know their true production, supplies, reserves, and profits. Those citizens who insist on driving large, unnecessarily powerful cars must expect to pay more for that luxury.

We can be sure that all the special interest groups in the country will attack the part of this plan that affects them directly. They will say that sacrifice is fine as long as other people do it, but that their sacrifice is unreasonable or unfair or harmful to the country. If they succeed with this approach, then the burden on the ordinary citizen, who it not organized into an interest group, would be crushing.

There should be only one test for this program— whether it will help our country. Other generations of Americans have faced and mastered great challenges. I have faith that meeting this challenge will make our own lives even richer. If you will join me so that we can work together with patriotism and courage, we will again prove that our great nation can lead the world into an age of peace, independence, and freedom.

Thank you very much, and good night.

HUMAN RIGHTS AND THE FOREIGN POLICY [3]

Cyrus R. Vance [4]

One of the key problems facing the Carter Administration is the conduct of foreign policy. One criticism leveled during the presidential campaign concerned the secrecy under which many of Secretary of State Henry A. Kissinger's negotiations were shrouded. Openly and repeatedly since his inauguration, President Carter has linked human rights with foreign policy. For example, before the United Nations on March 17, 1977, he stated:

> The search for peace and justice also means respect for human dignity. All the signatories of the UN Charter have pledged themselves to observe and to respect basic human rights. Thus, no member of the United Nations can claim that mistreatment of its citizens is solely its own business. Equally, no member can avoid its responsibilities to review and to speak when torture or unwarranted deprivation occurs in any part of the world.
>
> The basic thrust of human affairs points toward a more universal demand for fundamental human rights. The United States has a historical birthright to be associated with this process.
>
> We in the United States accept this responsibility in the fullest and the most constructive sense. Ours is a commitment, and not just a political posture. . . .
>
> Strengthened international machinery will help us to close the gap between promise and performance in protecting human rights. When gross or widespread violation takes place—contrary to international commitments—it is of concern to all. The solemn commitments of the United Nations Charter, of the United Nations Universal Declaration for Human Rights, of the Helsinki Accords, and of many other international instruments must be taken just as seriously as commercial or security agreements.

President Carter has made many other pronouncements on human rights. He has demonstrated his concern by personally

[3] Delivered during the observance of Law Day, at the Coliseum, University of Georgia, Athens, April 30, 1977.
[4] For biographical note, see Appendix.

meeting with Soviet dissident Vladimir Bukovsky, writing a letter to another dissident, Andrei Sakharov, and by seeking more
funds for Radio Free Europe and Radio Liberty. Russian leadership has reacted vehemently to President Carter's words and
actions. When Cyrus Vance, Secretary of State, carried a proposal
for arms reduction to Moscow, he was bluntly received and made
no progress. The affront was a blow to the Carter Administration at a time when it was attempting to assert itself internationally. In a two-hour speech in late March to the Soviet trade
unions in Moscow, Soviet leader Leonid Brezhnev frankly stated
his position:

> Washington's claims to teach others how to live, I be-
> lieve, cannot be accepted by any sovereign state. . . . We
> will not tolerate interference in our internal affairs by any-
> one and under any pretext. A normal development of
> relations on such a basis is, of course, unthinkable. [US-
> Soviet relations, he said, require] a definite level of mu-
> tual understanding and at least a minimum of mutual
> tact.

Many observers have seriously questioned the wisdom of Carter's openness with the American people on foreign policy and
his oversimplified pronouncements on human rights. They fear
that he will destroy detente and scheduled negotiations with the
Soviet Union. Reacting to Carter's eagerness to share his thoughts
on foreign policy with the American people, John Osborne (*New
Republic*, April 9, 1977) wrote: "In matters as delicate, as complex, as vital to human survival as strategic arms limitation is,
the President had better concentrate first upon effective communication with the adversary—in this instance the Soviet government—and only after that has been accomplished upon communication with his own people."

Obviously the Carter position on human rights and foreign
policy made necessary a carefully worded policy statement. Cyrus
Vance, Secretary of State, found such an opportunity when he
spoke on Law Day at the University of Georgia, April 30, 1977.
He addressed an immediate audience of students, faculty, and
alumni. On the platform with him were former Secretary of
State Dean Rusk (now a professor at Georgia), the Democratic
Senators from Georgia—Herman Talmadge and Sam Nunn—and
Governor George Busbee. The speech was broadcast by closed
circuit to reporters at the State Department in Washington, D.C.
It was broadcast live over the Voice of America through campus
radio station WUOG. A video tape of the speech will be dis-
tributed by the United States Information Agency to 115 coun-

tries. Anytime the United States Secretary of State speaks anywhere he has a worldwide audience. What he says comes under consideration in all foreign ministries. Likewise citizens in the free world look to him for leadership. Secretary Vance clearly set forth his goal, saying: "Our human rights policy must be understood in order to be effective. So today I want to set forth the substance of that policy, and the results we hope to achieve."

On the platform, Secretary of State Vance is a presence that commands respect. He is tall and slender, soft spoken and calm. *U.S. News & World Report* calls him a "highly professional diplomat, impeccable character" (April 18, 1977). Frank Stanton, retired president of CBS, once described him as "strong, thoughtful, experienced and courageous." After hearing the Law Day speech at Athens a reporter for the *University of Georgia Community News* (May 9, 1977), characterized Vance as speaking "calmly, dispassionately, but with subdued eloquence."

Dean Beaird, students, faculty and alumni of the University of Georgia Law School, distinguished guests: I am delighted to be here with you on Law Day. And I am honored by the presence of my friend Dean Rusk, a distinguished member of your faculty.

I speak today about the resolve of this Administration to make the advancement of human rights a central part of our foreign policy.

Many here today have long been advocates of human rights within our own society. And throughout our nation that struggle for civil rights continues.

In the early years of our civil rights movement, many Americans treated the issue as a "Southern" problem. They were wrong. It was and is a problem for all of us. Now, as a nation, we must not make a comparable mistake. Protection of human rights is a challenge for all countries, not just for a few.

Our human rights policy must be understood in order to be effective. So today I want to set forth the substance of that policy and the results we hope to achieve.

Our concern for human rights is built upon ancient values. It looks with hope to a world in which liberty is not just a great cause but the common condition. In the past it may have seemed sufficient to put our name to international documents that spoke loftily of human rights. That is not enough. We will go to work, alongside other people and governments, to protect and enhance the dignity of the individual.

Let me define what we mean by "human rights."

First, there is the right to be free from government violation of the integrity of the person. Such violations include torture; cruel, inhuman, or degrading treatment or punishment; and arbitrary arrest or imprisonment. And they include denial of fair public trial, and invasion of the home.

Second, there is the right to the fulfillment of such vital needs as food, shelter, health care, and education. We recognize that the fulfillment of this right will depend, in part, upon the stage of a nation's economic development. But we also know that this right can be violated by a government's action or inaction—for example, through corrupt official processes which divert resources to an elite at the expense of the needy, or through indifference to the plight of the poor.

Third, there is the right to enjoy civil and political liberties—freedom of thought, of religion, of assembly; freedom of speech; freedom of the press; freedom of movement both within and outside one's own country; freedom to take part in government.

Our policy is to promote all these rights. They are all recognized in the Universal Declaration of Human Rights, a basic document which the United States helped fashion and which the United Nations approved in 1948. There may be disagreement on the priorities these rights deserve, but I believe that, with work, all of these rights can become complementary and mutually reinforcing.

The philosophy of our human rights policy is revolutionary in the intellectual sense, reflecting our nation's origin and progressive values. As Archibald MacLeish wrote during our Bicentennial a year ago, "The cause of human liberty is now the one great revolutionary cause. . . ."

President Carter put it this way in his speech before the United Nations:

> . . . All the signatories of the United Nations Charter have pledged themselves to observe and to respect basic human rights. Thus, no member of the United Nations can claim that mistreatment of its citizens is solely its own business. Equally, no member can avoid its responsibilities to review and to speak when torture or unwarranted deprivation occurs in any part of the world. . . .

Since 1945 international practice has confirmed that a nation's obligations to respect human rights is a matter of concern in international law.

Our obligation under the UN Charter is written into our own legislation. For example, our Foreign Assistance Act now reads: "A principal goal of the foreign policy of the United States is to promote the increased observance of internationally recognized human rights by all countries." In these ways our policy is in keeping with our tradition, our international obligations, and our laws.

In pursuing a human rights policy, we must always keep in mind the limits of our power and of our wisdom. A sure formula for defeat of our goals would be a rigid, hubristic attempt to impose our values on others. A doctrinaire plan of action would be as damaging as indifference.

We must be realistic. Our country can only achieve our objectives if we shape what we do to the case at hand. In each instance we will consider these questions as we determine whether and how to act:

First, we will ask ourselves, what is the nature of the case that confronts us? For example, what kind of violations or deprivations are there? What is their extent? Is there a pattern to the violations? If so, is the trend toward concern for human rights or away from it? What is the degree of control and responsibility of the government involved? And, finally, is the government willing to permit independent, outside investigation?

A *second* set of questions concerns the prospects for effective action. Will our action be useful in promoting the overall cause of human rights? Will it actually improve the specific conditions at hand? Or will it be likely to make things worse instead? Is the country involved receptive to our interest and efforts? Will others work with us, including official and private international organizations dedicated to furthering human rights? Finally does our sense of values and decency demand that we speak out or take action anyway, even though there is only a remote chance of making our influence felt?

We will ask a *third* set of questions in order to maintain a sense of perspective. Have we steered away from the self-righteous and strident, remembering that our own record is not unblemished? Have we been sensitive to genuine security interests, realizing that outbreak of armed conflict or terrorism could in itself pose a serious threat to human rights? Have we considered all the rights at stake? If, for instance, we reduce aid to a government which violates the political rights of its citizens, do we not risk penalizing the hungry and poor who bear no responsibility for the abuses of their government?

If we are determined to act, the means available range from quiet diplomacy in its many forms through public pronouncements to withholding of assistance. Whenever possible, we will use positive steps of encouragement and inducement. Our strong support will go to countries that are working to improve the human condition. We will always try to act in concert with other countries through international bodies.

In the end a decision whether and how to act in the cause of human rights is a matter for informed and careful judgment. No mechanistic formula produces an automatic answer.

It is not our purpose to intervene in the internal affairs of other countries, but as the President has emphasized, no member of the United Nations can claim that violation of internationally protected human rights is solely its own affair. It is our purpose to shape our policies in accord with our beliefs and to state them without stridency or apology when we think it is desirable to do so.

Our policy is to be applied within our own society as well as abroad. We welcome constructive criticism at the same time as we offer it.

No one should suppose that we are working in a vacuum. We place great weight on joining with others in the cause of human rights. The UN system is central to this cooperative endeavor. That is why the President stressed the pursuit of human rights in his speech before the General Assembly last month. That is why he is calling for US ratification of four important human rights covenants and conventions, and why we are trying to strengthen the human rights machinery within the United Nations.

And that is an important reason why we have moved to comply with UN sanctions against Rhodesia. In one of our first acts, this Administration sought and achieved repeal of the Byrd amendment, which had placed us in violation of these sanctions and thus in violation of international law. We are supporting other diplomatic efforts within the United Nations to promote basic civil and political rights in Namibia and throughout southern Africa.

Regional organizations also play a central role in promoting human rights. The President has announced that the United States will sign and seek Senate approval of the American Convention on Human Rights. We will continue to work to strengthen the machinery of the Inter-American Commission on Human Rights. This will include efforts to schedule regular visits to all members of the Organization of American States, annual debates on human rights conditions, and the expansion of the inter-American educational program on human rights.

The United States is seeking increased consultation with other nations for joint programs on economic assistance and more general efforts to promote human rights. We are working to assure that our efforts reach out to all, with particular sensitivity to the problems of women.

We will meet in Belgrade later this year to review implementation of the Final Act of the Conference on Security and Cooperation in Europe—the so-called Helsinki conference. We will take this occasion to work for progress there on important human issues: family reunification, binational marriages, travel for personal and professional reasons, and freer access to information.

The United States looks to use of economic assistance—whether bilateral or through international financial institutions—as a means to foster basic human rights.

☐ We have proposed a 20 percent increase in US foreign economic assistance for Fiscal Year 1978.

☐ We are expanding the program of the Agency for International Development for "new initiatives in human rights" as a complement to present efforts to get the benefits of our aid to those most in need abroad.

☐ The programs of the US Information Agency and the State Department's Bureau of Educational and Cultural Affairs stress support for law in society, a free press, freedom of communication, an open educational system, and respect for ethnic diversity.

This Administration's human rights policy has been framed in collaboration and consultation with Congress and private organizations. We have taken steps to assure firsthand contact, consultation, and observation when members of Congress travel abroad to review human rights conditions.

We are implementing current laws that bring human rights considerations directly into our decisions in several international financial institutions. At the same time, we are working with the Congress to find the most effective way to fulfill our parallel commitment to international cooperation in economic development.

In accordance with human rights provisions of legislation governing our security assistance programs, we recently announced cuts in military aid to several countries.

Outside the government, there is much that can be done. We welcome the efforts of individual American citizens and private organizations—such as religious, humanitarian, and professional groups—to work for human rights with commitments of time, money, and compassion.

All these initiatives to further human rights abroad would have a hollow ring if we were not prepared to improve our own performance at home. So we have removed all restrictions on our citizens' travel abroad and are proceeding with plans to liberalize our visa policies.

We support legislation and administrative action to expand our refugee and asylum policies and to permit more victims of repressive regimes to enter the United States. During this last year, the United States spent some $475 million on assistance to refugees around the world, and we accepted 31,000 refugees for permanent resettlement in this country.

What results can we expect from all these efforts?

We may justifiably seek a rapid end to such gross violations as those cited in our law: ". . . torture, or cruel, inhuman or degrading treatment or punishment, or prolonged detention without charges. . . ." Just last week our Ambassador at the United Nations, Andrew Young, suggested a series of new ways to confront the practice of torture around the world.

The promotion of other human rights is a broader challenge. The results may be slower in coming but are no less worth pursuing, and we intend to let other countries know where we stand.

We recognize that many nations of the world are organized on authoritarian rather than democratic principles —some large and powerful, others struggling to raise the lives of their people above bare subsistence levels. We can nourish no illusions that a call to the banner of human rights will bring sudden transformations in authoritarian societies.

We are embarked on a long journey. But our faith in the dignity of the individual encourages us to believe that people in every society, according to their own traditions, will in time give their own expression to this fundamental aspiration.

Our belief is strengthened by the way the Helsinki principles and the UN Declaration of Human Rights have found resonance in the hearts of people of many countries. Our task is to sustain this faith by our example and our encouragement.

In his inaugural address, three months ago, President Carter said: "Because we are free, we can never be indifferent to the fate of freedom elsewhere." Again, at a meeting of the Organization of American States two weeks ago, he said: "You will find this country . . . eager to stand beside those nations which respect human rights and which promote democratic ideals."

We seek these goals because they are right, and because we too will benefit. Our own well-being, and even our security, are enhanced in a world that shares common freedoms and in which prosperity and economic justice create the conditions for peace. And let us remember that we always risk paying a serious price when we become identified with repression.

Nations, like individuals, limit their potential when they limit their goals. The American people understand this. I am confident they will support foreign policies that reflect our traditional values. To offer less is to define America in ways we should not accept.

America fought for freedom in 1776 and in two world wars. We have offered haven to the oppressed. Millions have come to our shores in times of trouble. In time of devastation abroad, we have shared our resources.

Our encouragement and inspiration to other nations and other peoples have never been limited to the power of our military or the bounty of our economy. They have been lifted up by the message of our Revolution, the message of individual human freedom. That message has been our great national asset in times past. So it should be again.

OF MIND AND SPIRIT

BEGINNINGS [1]

DANIEL J. BOORSTIN [2]

On November 9, 1976, Daniel J. Boorstin, Librarian of Congress, addressed 150 persons gathered for dinner in the Great Hall of the Library of Congress. The occasion marked the opening of the exhibition entitled "Beginnings," an exhibit of 35 treasures from the collection of the Library of Congress displayed in the Great Hall as landmarks in the exploration of ideas and places. The distinguished gathering included members of Congress, the Chief Justice of the United States, government officials, and great friends of the Library of Congress, such as Lessing J. Rosenwald, donor of "priceless incunabula and other rare books" (information supplied by Mary C. Lethbridge, information officer of the Library of Congress).

In a brochure describing the exhibition, Daniel Boorstin wrote:

> "A good man," observed the ancient Roman moralist, "is always a beginner." Great beginnings dramatize our powers of renewal.
>
> In our age countless items proceed from novelty to obsolescence without ever having become new beginnings. Hula-Hoops and Edsels obsolesce without innovating. Annual models, overnight sensations, are not necessarily beginnings. Eventually, if not recycled, they disfigure and obstruct our landscape. But the epoch-markers and epoch-makers—the accumulating works of intellectual beginnings from all past ages—brighten our vistas and widen our vision. . . .
>
> Here at the Library of Congress it is our joyful assignment to put it all in perspective, to allow the works of our age to enrich all that has come before, and to set side-by-side the illusory and the real new beginnings so that each of us can judge for himself. Literature, as Ezra

---

[1] Delivered in the Great Hall of the Library of Congress, Washington, D.C., November 9, 1976. Quoted by permission.
[2] For biographical note, see Appendix.

Pound once remarked, is news that stays news. Here it is our mission to see that the old stays new.

Simple and direct, the speech is eloquent in its composition and theme, a splendid example of a speech of communication. It reaches a high point when the speaker says in his concluding sentences:

> We must provide here a fellowship of adventuring learners. We must, in this very building, provide a beautiful, congenial home where explorers can delight in one another's work, exchanging tales of their adventures. This can be an explorers' club open to all.
> Here is a great treasury of the known, but an even richer treasury of the unknown. We must find new ways to help each of us, each American, learn again and again to be a beginner.

Our theme tonight is beginnings. We can never be sure when we have seen one, when there has been one, or when there will be one. The origin of this robust Anglo-Saxon word is itself shrouded in mystery. *Begin* seems to have the same root as that from which we get our word *to yawn*. Yawning, too, is a kind of opening.

Beginnings have always inspired awe. The Bible begins with "in the beginning," and "in the beginning was the Word." Everything is a beginning, though it has taken most of human history to make this discovery. To discover this truth is to discover history—that the life of our species is not mere repetition, but is full of novelty, full of beginnings. The capacity for beginnings makes us human and keeps us human.

The exhibition which opens this evening will help us grasp and witness again and again the mystery of beginnings. In the *natural* world if we know the seed we can predict the fruit. But, never in our human world—the world of thought and science and art. What makes our beginnings human is precisely their unpredictability. Copernicus would bear an exotic harvest—new religious sects, a new sense of time, a new universe of travel. Emerson's encouraging letter to Whitman and Whitman's own new accents fructified a new sense of what was American, a new sense of the poetic. The human miracle, which we celebrate here tonight —perhaps what those have meant who say that God created man in his own image—is that man seems able to create new kinds of everything.

Here, with these treasures spread before us, we can learn to distinguish the real beginning from the annual model. In our age countless items proceed from novelty to obsolescence without ever having become new beginnings. Hula-hoops and Edsels obsolesce without innovating. Overnight sensations, headline makers, full-page-ad fillers are not necessarily beginnings. Today as never before we need a place like the Library of Congress where we can distinguish the debris of still unrecycled annual models which only disfigure the landscape—from the epoch-markers and epoch-makers, the accumulating works of intellectual beginnings from all past ages, which can brighten our vistas and widen our vision.

This Library is a treasury of beginnings. Here we can sample their mysteries and their promise. What beginnings are most fertile of other beginnings? How does Samuel de Champlain's map of northeastern America, or Alexander Graham Bell's telephone, or Sigmund Freud's idea of the subconscious, or Albert Einstein's concept of space-time relations—how do all these become opening chapters for later adventures into the unknown?

Ours is not a teaching institution. But it is a learning institution. Successful teaching imposes special limitations. There must be a curriculum with disciplined channels of study—and then tests of achievement, and badges of achievement, grades and honors and degrees. Teaching institutions obviously depend on teachers whose services are irregular and discontinuous, whose teachings are channeled and curricularized. Teachers are mortal, they seek better posts elsewhere, they go on vacation, they lose their elastic step, their clear, articulate voice. The stimulus of the classroom depends, too, on the qualities of fellow-students.

A *learning* institution like ours does not provide the teacher, the curriculum, or the classmates. Our opportunities are not narrowed by a curriculum nor by the rhetoric of any particular professor. Our offerings do not vary with the season, the semester, or the sabbaticals of the teaching staff.

Here in this *learning* institution, the learner—call him a student or whatever you will—is supreme. His interests and desires, even his whims, *are* the curriculum. Here everyman makes his own university.

We are the most traditional of educational institutions. We offer the classics, the great books, the heritage of learning. Yet we are the most progressive of educational institutions. John Dewey need not preach here. We already open vistas of uninhibited self-discovery. Here the only complaint of the learner may be that of the proverbial progressive school student, "Do I really *have* to do what I want to do?"

In a country of great teaching institutions how can we make this the best possible learning institution? Congress and the American people have endowed us here with learning resources unexampled in human history, unparalleled in the world today. Our collections of books and periodicals, of maps and atlases, of photographs and the graphic arts, of motion pictures, of musical recordings, musical scores and librettos, incunabula and rare books, manuscripts, Braille books and talking books—each of these collections shine by comparison with any similar collection past or present.

We reach into all past ages and touch all nations on all continents. Here we get the word from ancient Egypt and Chaldea, from earliest China and Korea and Greece and Rome. Here we learn not only about Islam and Christianity and Judaism, but also about Buddhism and Shinto and Tao, about tribal religions and how people have sought and found their gods.

Our unexcelled collections about everything American—our culture, our literature, our economy, our geography, our politics, our technology, our science, our achievements and frustrations in war and in peace—make us a national library. We are a national library too, by our service to all the nation's libraries. Over three quarters of a century we have distributed more than 2 billion 200 million cards, along with immeasurable economies of time and money, and other benefits that reach to the smallest libraries in the remote corners of our nation. During this period we have actively shared our resources through some seven million interlibrary loans.

Of course, our primary function is to be the Congress' and the nation's library. It is less noted that in a sense, we are also the world's library. We have *had* to become an international library in order to serve the needs of the Congress and of the nation, in order to be a truly national library for the United States in the twentieth century. This year we Americans have been reminded again and again, that we are, in Whitman's words, a nation of nations. "Our blood is as the flood of the Amazon," Melville explained, "made up of a thousand noble currents all pouring into one. We are not a nation, so much as a world." It may suffice for national libraries of other nations to confine their major collections to their own language and their limited territory. If we are to be a national library for these United States we have no choice but to be worldwide in our interests, catholic, multilingual, fully human in our collections. It should not be surprising, then, that some two thirds of our 17.5 million books, of our total of 80 million items, are in languages other than English. In this library we catalog in some 468 languages. The competence of our staff now reaches some 120 living languages. This kind of congressional library has required an outreach to people in far places. Keeping these comprehensive collections up to date —in the service of the Congress, of scholars, and of an enlightened citizenry—requires that our staff be versatile, vigilant, efficient, enterprising, and imaginative.

Of course, we have our problems. Problems of space. Where to put and how best to preserve our accumulating treasures. Problems of service. How to find promptly from our millions the one particular item wanted by a member of Congress, by a scholar, by any interested reader here, or by the reader in another library. We are working at these and other problems with the aid of an able task force from our staff and of advisory groups from the whole nation. Our problems are the price of our prosperity.

Our problems come from the vast extent of our treasure, from its constant increase. We receive one and one half items every working second, and we would not have it otherwise. Our problems come also from the welcome, ever-increasing demands of a nation of learners. Our problems, like our treasures, are a measure of our opportunities.

Now we will have the new opportunity to draw together collections from a dozen locations into the magnificent James Madison Building across the street. We will remove the unsightly partitions which have defaced this building, will provide our staff with a more acceptable working environment and finally will give the treasures now crowded into this building the living-space they need and deserve. At long last we can restore this grand building to its intended grandeur—the grandeur of civilization itself.

In our new age this building, the symbolic heart of our library, will play a special role. Details for the fulfillment of our hopes will have to be worked out under the guidance and in close consultation with the Joint Committee of the Congress, in collaboration with the inspired architect of the Capitol and his able staff, in cooperation with the nationwide communities of our constituents, and, of course, with the peerless staff of the library.

In a nation replete with great and effective centers of teaching, what are the special—not only the residual, but the unique and remarkable—roles of this grand center of learning?

These past decades in the United States have seen the multiplication of schools and colleges and universities, of learned societies and specialized publications. In my own field of history alone we see countless new societies and new journals—for interdisciplinary history, for psycho-history, for cliometrics, along with periodicals focused on the needs and problems, the arts and literature and economy and politics of every part of the world. New "disciplines," new categories of information, new ways of gathering facts, and then of interrelating facts in one category to those in another— all these multiply with the seasons.

World War II more than any world event before dramatized the crucial place of research and development in the nation's survival. R&D entered our jargon. Research institutes have multiplied. The first known national estimate of trends in expenditure for research and development was made by Dr. Vannevar Bush as recently as 1945. The first such figures appear in our Historical Statistics (Bureau of Census) in 1953, when funds expended in the USA for Research and Development amounted to $5.2 billion. By 1970 the figure reached 26.5 billion (55 percent were federal funds). The titles of books published in the United States increased from some eleven thousand in 1950 to some forty thousand this year. Every year, the new periodicals started somewhere in the world number about seventeen thousand. And I have not even mentioned that for any single year (1970 for example) there may be copyrighted as many as eighty-odd thousand musical compositions, two thousand maps, twenty-five hundred motion picture films, along with thousands of still photographs, and miscellaneous other items which must be counted among sources of knowledge.

This overwhelming bulk has led other institutions to become increasingly selective. Inflation and lack of community support have forced libraries to limit their scope. But even our best efforts to help other libraries meet their financial needs will not enable them to be fully comprehensive in their collections. Their limits and their specialization inevitably mean the separation of one kind of knowledge from another.

We must not allow our nation's success, our intellectual

ferment and creativity irreparably to fragment our culture. Someone somewhere must make the effort to be comprehensive. Where is that place?

It is here! Certain parts of this task have been undertaken by the National Library of Medicine and the National Agricultural Library. But the essential task of comprehensiveness remains ours, right here in the Library of Congress. For decades we have been working at this assignment, and have, on the whole, been remarkably successful.

We must be fertile and comprehensive, not only in our collections, but in our use of our treasures. We must enlist more scholars to explore here. We must have a Center for the Book to help us understand the history of the book and the place of the book in history. The Engelhard lectures on the Book, begun this year, are a new start. We must be a nursery of scholarship and music, and the graphic arts. We must find ways to display them—by traveling exhibits and other means—to perform them, and to encourage their performance. We must be a home for a comprehensive American culture for the benefit of Americans everywhere.

In this increasingly necessary, ever-more-urgent task this Library of Congress Building is our focus. This, our central building will be our encyclopedia. *Encyclopaedia* originally meant the circle of knowledge of the arts and sciences essential to a liberal education. An encyclopaedia, in Sir Thomas Browne's phrase, offers "the round of knowledge." For this purpose the shape of our grand reading room, which I would like to christen the Hall of Knowledge, is not merely symbolic. It will be functional. From our central Hall of Knowledge any serious comer should be able to survey the sweep of knowledge—to see vistas in all directions. From here the learner will be guided into more specialized learning rooms, some (on this floor) for particular disciplines—the social sciences, the humanities, the physical sciences—some (on the floor above) for particular civilizations, defined by language and by geographic area. And then on to our vast specialized collections—on economics, on Orientalia, on aeronautics—where he can settle down to work in depth. At each of these points we hope to aid him with human guides from the widely and deeply learned staff of this library who know the intellectual landscape because they have been there themselves.

Earlier ages have been oppressed by ignorance. It would be ironic if ours should be victimized by the excess of knowledge. Our library exists to help us prevent that unnecessary tragedy. Therefore, we must provide not only an encyclopaedia, but an index. We must not only help any willing person to survey the wilderness of knowledge, we must help him find his way.

This central Hall of Knowledge must be a headquarters for exploration. There the learner seeks a guide, from there he will be introduced to others of our great corps of guides elsewhere in the library. The central Hall of Knowledge will provide not merely the traditional apparatus of catalog cards, but the magical new apparatus of the computer, to offer the most modern most usable index to the knowledge of all times and places.

Today the drift of American civilization must impress on us the need for instructions where Americans may explore for themselves. Even while knowledge is extended and while our arts become more adventurous and more varied, the channels of popular communication (which dominate our lives more than ever) somehow become narrower. While colleges offer us "curricula" (a word appropriately derived from Latin *currere*, to run, as along a race-course) which change with the seasons, broadcasting offers us channels. Competition on the airwaves—a hallmark of our free society —seems itself to reduce the reality and the range of our choices. Every season there seems less difference between what the different channels offer us.

Meanwhile, in the world of book publishing, the annually increasing titles make us desperate to escape from the bewildering multitude of apparent choices, and so dig deeper the channels of best-sellerdom. The pressures toward

celebrity—in books, as in people—become ever more overwhelming. Just as the celebrity-person who dominates our
news is someone well-known for his well-knownness, so too
the celebrity-book which dominates our reviewing media
sells because it is (or is reputed to be) a best-seller.

Our world of channels needs this library. Libraries remain islands of choice in a world of channels. And this great
Library of Congress is a vast continent of choices.

We can remain a temple of autonomy, where the free
autonomous individual can think and explore and read and
see and hear as he wishes. Those who still wish to swim in
the swiftly changing currents of best-sellerdom can do so
here. Those who wish to become refugees from an over-
channelled world can find their refuge here. Those who wish
to grasp the latest fragment of news or the newest information in literature, in politics, in economics, in the sciences,
can find those fragments here. Those who wish to reach
back across the channels and across the centuries can delight
in the world that was news to Copernicus or Champlain or
Alexander Graham Bell or Orville Wright. Those who wish
to enjoy the latest product—in maps, in photographs, in
movies, in prints, in phonograph recordings and tape-record-
ings—find their treasure here. So, too, those who wish to
enjoy a page of Caxton, a Beethoven manuscript, a print
by Blake, a medieval Book of Hours.

Some of our opportunities for new beginnings are dramatized here tonight in the exhibition which surrounds us.
This building was intended to be not only an encyclopedia,
an index to civilization and civilizations, but a showplace
for the human, and especially the American, achievement.
With the opportunities now offered us—foreshadowed in
the renovation (I almost said the "denovation") of this great
hall and the circumambient halls—we will witness a renais-
sance of our exhibits, a grand reopening of our American
treasury. We want more Americans to come here to see what
they did not know was their own. Our exhibits will, we
hope, be irresistible appetizers. We will try to make them

as dramatic, as enticing (as suggested by the invitations each of us received for this evening), as our wondrous treasures deserve.

We must point the way from everyone's special territory to all neighboring territories. We must keep the frontiers open so that people can freely move back and forth—without need for tuition, entrance examination, or other academic passport—from the world of incunabula to the world of news, from books to maps, from the printed word to the imprinted image and the recorded sound.

This central building, we hope, will be, more than ever before, a place of beginnings for millions of voyages of exploration and discovery, each uniquely designed by and for each new explorer. Here is the point of departure for countless expeditions—each a party of one. This building is the new Independence—like the old Independence, Missouri—from which every intellectual pioneer can find and move into his very own new West.

We must provide here a fellowship of adventuring learners. We must, in this very building, provide a beautiful, congenial home where explorers can delight in one another's work, exchanging tales of their adventures. This can be an explorers' club open to all.

Here is a great treasury of the known, but an even richer treasury of the unknown. We must find new ways to help each of us, each American, learn again and again to be a beginner.

"LET CANDLES BE BROUGHT" [3]

Sol M. Linowitz [4]

On March 8, 1977, Sol M. Linowitz, a prominent lawyer, received the Charles E. Wilson Memorial Award of the Religion in American Life organization at the annual dinner held in the Grand Ballroom of the Waldorf-Astoria Hotel, New York City. The audience consisted of leaders in business, the professions, education, government, and various religious groups of the nation. RIAL, as it is known to its supporters, embraces forty-three cooperating religious groups and is supported by numerous corporations.

The occasion was serious and inspirational and demanded a response fitting the purpose and the mood. Linowitz suggested that Americans dedicate themselves "to the fulfillment of our mission as a beacon of hope for ourselves and for the other people of this world . . . drawing upon the richness within our faiths." The speech pivots on the idea that we are our brother's keepers.

In his introduction Linowitz appropriately minimizes the honor bestowed upon him with his opening story. This enables him to shift full attention to his main theme. It is an effective introduction. He then develops the premise that the moment is "uncertain, fearful and indeed dangerous," spending almost half of the speech in amplification of the seriousness of this "threat" and "challenge."

In the second half of the speech he turns to a consideration of "two diametrically opposed philosophies" that offer "a longer slice of bread" to "the people of this earth." After succinctly characterizing what Communism promises, he presents an eloquent plea for the tenets of Democracy. In his final ten paragraphs he synthesizes the facets of the freedom myth that was given force in the Declaration of Independence and in the great American speeches of the nineteenth and twentieth centuries. The last sentences bring the speech to a spirited close.

As I look around this room and see so many who have

---

[3] Delivered at the annual dinner of Religion in American Life, Waldorf-Astoria Hotel, New York City, March 8, 1977. Award jointly sponsored by Religion in American Life and General Electric Company. Quoted by permission.

[4] For biographical note, see Appendix.

done so much over the years for so many, I must admit
that I have a sense of kinship with William Howard Taft's
great-granddaughter who in her third-grade autobiography
wrote: "My great-grandfather was President of the United
States, my grandfather was a United States Senator, my
father is an ambassador, and I am a Brownie."

I want you to know that in your presence, I am a
Brownie.

I am truly grateful to you for the award this evening,
for the spirit in which you have tendered it, and for the
auspices under which you have presented it. Let me express
my special appreciation to the General Electric Company for
the generous contribution which they have made on my
behalf in the name of that distinguished American, Charles
E. Wilson.

With your permission I would like to take a few minutes
just to say a few things which are on my mind and my heart.

We are met at a moment in history which is uncertain,
fearful and indeed, dangerous. While it is true as Professor
Whitehead once said that "it is the business of the future
to be dangerous," nonetheless there is reason for concern
as we look about us.

We are at a time that has been called both the Age of
Anxiety and the Age of Science and Technology. Both are
accurate, for indeed one feeds upon the other. As our scientific and technological competence has increased, so have
our fear and anxiety.

In a real sense we are at a time of paradox—a time when
we have learned to achieve most and to fear most. It is a
time when we seem to know much more about how to make
war than how to make peace, more about killing than we
do about living. It is a time of unprecedented need and unparalleled plenty, a time when great advances in medicine
and science and technology are overshadowed by incredible
achievements in instruments of destruction. It is a time
when the world fears not the primitive or the ignorant man,

but the educated, the technically competent man, who has it in his power to destroy civilization.

It is a time when malaise hangs heavy, when we can send men up to walk the moon yet hauntingly recall Santayana's words that people have come to power who "having no stomach for the ultimate, burrow themselves downward toward the primitive."

No one needs to remind us that this moment may be the most fateful in all the long history of mankind. And that the outcome will depend on whether the human intellect which has invented such total instruments of destruction, can now develop ways of peace that will keep any man, no matter what his ideology, his race or his nation, from pushing the fatal button.

In the past men have warred over frontiers, they have come into conflict over ideologies. And they have fought over ideologies. And they have fought to better their daily lives. But today each crisis seems to overlap the other and we are engaged in a vast human upheaval that touches upon every phase of our existence—national and international, religious and racial.

Part of that upheaval is as old as hunger. Part is as new as a walk in lunar space. The overriding fact is that today we are all part of a global society in which there no longer is any such thing as a separate or isolated concern, in which peace is truly indivisible.

And the fact is that whether we like it or not, either we will all survive together or none of us will. Either we will all share the world's bounty, or none of us will.

We must, therefore, ask what chance we have of accepting our shrinking world with its fewer and fewer natural frontiers, or of transcending our ideological struggles unless we are prepared finally to get to the roots of the problem—the roots that are dug so deep in injustice and resentment in a worldwide contrast between wealth and misery. And the answers are vital not only to a sound foreign policy, but to a compassionate domestic policy. Indeed, both are interrelated in an interdependent world. For there is no escape any longer from what I believe is surely the central fact of our time: That whether it be Africa or Asia or Latin America or New York or Detroit or Washington—human beings can no longer be condemned to hunger and disease and to the indignity of a life without hope.

Who are these human beings that make up this world in which we live—the millions upon millions no longer thousands of miles away, but not just down the runway? Here they are in microcosm: During the next 60 seconds, 200 human beings will be born on this earth. About 160 of them will be black, brown, yellow or red. Of these 200 youngsters now being born, about half will be dead before they are a year old. Of those that survive, another half will be dead before they are sixteen. The 50 of the 200 who live past their sixteenth birthday, multiplied by thousands and millions, represent the people of this earth.

They, like their fathers and forefathers before them, will till the soil working for landlords, living in tents or mud huts. Most of them will never learn to read or write. Most of them will be poor and tired and hungry most of their lives. Most of them—like their fathers and their forefathers—will lie under the open skies of Asia, Africa and Latin America watching, waiting, hoping. These are our brothers and sisters, our fellow human beings on this earth.

What kind of a tomorrow does the world offer these, the people of this earth? Two diametrically opposed philosophies are being presented. One we call Communism—the other Democracy. Each asks acceptance of a basic idea; each offers a larger slice of bread.

Make common cause with us, say the Communists, and accept three basic premises: First, *dialectical materialism*—all that matters is matter itself. Second, *godlessness*—accept the notion that there is no spiritual being who determines your destiny. Third, accept the idea that the *State is supreme* and determines the will of the individual. Believe these things and accept them, say the Communists, and we promise you more food in your stomachs, more clothes on your backs, a firmer roof over your heads.

And what about Democracy? Because Democracy rejects absolutes, it tends also to resist precise definition. But when you and I think of Democracy, we think of a system dedicated to the preservation of the *integrity, dignity* and *decency* of the individual person.

We talk of all men being created equal but what we really mean is that all men are created with an equal right to become unequal—to achieve the glorious inequality of their individual talent, their individual capacity, their individual genius. We don't talk of the common man because what we believe in is not man as common, but with a common right to become uncommon—to think uncommon thoughts, to believe uncommon beliefs, to be an uncommon man.

We like to say that in a Democracy every person has a right to life, a right to a decent life, which comes not from government, not from his fellow citizens, but from God. We say that in a Democracy it is the individual who matters; and because we count by ones and not by masses or by mobs, we believe that in a Democracy each human being, regardless of his race, his creed, his color, has the right—the God-given right—to stand erect with dignity as a child of God.

I submit to you that that is the essence of what we really mean when we talk about the impact of religion on American life—our deep faith in *every man's* right to stand erect and with dignity as a child of God. That is the basic principle to which we are committed as a nation and as a people; that is the foundation on which our system rests; and that is what distinguishes us in the eyes of the world—in the eyes of the world—in the eyes of those millions who are searching for hope of a better *future*.

From the beginning there has been an expectation about us as a nation. From the beginning the world has looked to us to live up to certain standards of integrity, decency, dignity and humanity—to involve ourselves deeply in moving humankind toward a more humane world of freedom and justice.

Archibald MacLeish once wrote: "America is promises." America is, indeed, promises. We started with a promise over two hundred years ago. At the time when we were but a loose group of weak and scattered colonies of 3 million people, we lit up the western sky with a promise based on faith and hope—the promise of a free and compassionate society committed to the preservation of fundamental human values.

From the beginning we have always treasured the human and the humane and we have always cared about what happened to other human beings. The promise we held out to the world—saying we did so "out of a decent respect to the opinions of mankind"—is still the promise of America to the millions on this earth.

And today as never before in our history we have the opportunity to redeem that promise. Today we have the science and the technology, the skills and the resources to make it happen, to put an end to the hunger and disease and privation that have for so long been the scourge of mankind.

The question is whether we have the will, whether we are prepared to do what we should and must if we are to be the kind of nation we have said we are.

We have a great responsibility to ourselves, to our heritage and to our children. We are not going to discharge that responsibility by building larger missiles or making more powerful warheads. We will not do it by issuing new and eloquent statements. We will only do it by remembering who we are and what we are—by tapping the very deepest within us as a people—by dedicating ourselves to the fulfillment of our mission as a beacon of hope for ourselves and for the other people of this world, not only as Americans but also as Christians and Jews, drawing upon the richest within our faiths.

As I indicated earlier, this is a time of uncertainty, of deep concern. But there is a moment in our history which I think suggests the temper in which we must approach whatever challenge is before us. On May 19, 1780, the Connecticut State Legislature was in session. For days there had been prophecies that it was to be the day of doom. Then suddenly in mid-morning the sky turned from blue to grey to black. Men fell on their knees in fear and in prayer and there were many shouts for adjournment. Then a state Senator, Abraham Davenport, came forward to the podium, banged the gavel and said, "Gentlemen, either the day of judgment is approaching or it is not. If it is not, then there is no need to adjourn, and if it is, I choose to be found doing my duty. I therefore ask, let candles be brought".

I suggest this is a time for all of us to make that commitment. Let us also determine that no matter what lies ahead we will be found doing our duty to God and our country. Let us together ask that candles be brought.

THE USES OF ADVERSITY [5]

GLENN A. CROSBY [6]

There is mounting evidence that while the quality of college students has decreased grades have been inflated. Pressure to grant every student "his rights" has brought pressure to let the inferior student slip through and to let many trade school courses satisfy degree requirements. Recruiting students often has involved high-powered salesmanship. Ewald B. Nyquist, president of the University of the State of New York, observed on March 10, 1977, at the Regents Twelfth Trustee Conference, in New York City:

> What we have . . . in some cases . . . are meretricious practices that amount to educational prostitution. The serpent of academic shoddiness is slipping into the basket of shiny apples. . . . It means there are colleges that are making programs sound better than they are and are promising more than they can deliver. They are beating the bushes for tuition-paying students, using hucksterism, slick advertising, and unethical, if not illegal, come-ons to pump up sagging enrollments.

The plight of academe provided Dr. Glenn A. Crosby, professor of chemistry at Washington State University, with the subject for his address at the annual initiation banquet of Phi Kappa Phi, an honor society for graduate students, March 8, 1976. He spoke to 243 initiates and approximately 100 others, including officers, faculty members, friends, and relatives, assembled in the Grand Ballroom of the Compton Union Building on campus. The response to Professor Crosby was strong and enthusiastic.

When the address was subsequently published in the *Phi Kappa Phi Journal,* the editor introduced it with the following headnote:

> Pleas for "academic excellence" have been received in such numbers in the past few years that they are rapidly

[5] Delivered at the annual initiation banquet of Phi Kappa Phi, Grand Ballroom, the Compton Union Building, Washington State University, Pullman, March 8, 1976. Published with Professor Crosby's documentation in *Phi Kappa Phi Journal,* Fall 1976, vol. 56, p 3-8. Quoted by permission.

[6] For biographical note, see Appendix.

becoming a glut on the market, and those who run the *Journal* have seriously considered running a plea to contributors not to send any more of them. Then came the manuscript of this address, and now we are glad we didn't. Read it, and we think you'll see what we mean.

This address demonstrates the characteristics of good speech composition. Organizing his material around a problem and its solution, Professor Crosby has assembled meaningful and striking facts. His language is dramatic. For example, he caustically says, "The student is lazy. We have grade inflation. While the achievements go down the gpa (grade point average) goes up. . . . The charade goes on. If the trend continues soon we will have most of the graduating class at this banquet. Then we will have created the ultimate in academic irony, an Honor Society without honor." In his solution he pointedly has "recommendations" for the faculty and for the students. The analogy between the Cathedral of St. Sophia and contemporary education provides a striking introduction and effective conclusion. When he returns to the analogy in his last paragraph he unifies his entire speech and concludes on a high note.

Accepting challenge is my business. I am a scientist and know that there is no more spirited adversary than nature when she guards her secrets. I viewed the task of speaking before this group as a challenge also and instantly accepted the invitation. But every challenge involves risk. I will now risk making some of you uncomfortable, others angry, a few of you depressed. Hopefully I risk shaking your complacence. I take the risk willingly; for there is much I would like to "get off my chest."

When pressed for a title some weeks ago, I had just had occasion to consult one of my favorite books, H. J. Muller's, *The Uses of the Past*. I had read it, as a student, over twenty years ago, and ever since that time it has occupied an honored place on my bookshelf. In it the author, a professor, English, describes his personal search for knowledge of the human condition. He proceeds by delving into the past. He begins by describing that great monument of Byzantine culture, the Cathedral of St. Sophia. When viewed from afar, both physically and historically, the cathedral gives the impression of otherworldly perfection, but, upon close inspection, this impression quickly vanishes. Within its corpus the cathedral hides shoddy workmanship, hasty structural shortcuts, and poorly disguised inferior building blocks. Much of its history is laced with brutality and the worst manifestations of cultural rottenness. In short, it is a very human construction. Nonetheless, it has stood for over a thousand years.

What struck me as I reread the book were some obvious parallels between the building of the Cathedral of St. Sophia and the development of the modern university, particularly those institutions, such as Washington State University, that have grown explosively during the last few decades. The cathedral was built in a hurry, a mere six years; little wonder that the workmen cut corners. It was dedicated to God but was quite clearly a personal triumph of the Emperor Justinian. The cathedral still stands, but everything is wavering, bulging, or askew. Most modern universities have a similar history. They have grown fast, too fast, and many corners have been cut. Although dedicated to education, scholarship, and research, they often developed in directions dictated by political, social, and economic pressures, directions sometimes perpendicular to the intended course. They stand, some of them quite well, but much is wavering, bulging, askew.

Wars and historical events finally overtook St. Sophia. In fact, it became a mosque, and then a museum. It still stands, but it certainly is not the same. Now, events are overtaking the modern university. After years of adjusting to growth pressures, social pressures, political pressures, and depreciating self-analysis, the modern university is confused. An identity crisis, we say. And on top of it all, a financial crunch. Misery, misery! Adversity is upon us. But just as there are "Uses of the Past," there are also "Uses of Adversity." Adversity is here, and we must cope with it. The question is, "Can we turn elements of adversity to our advantage?" We had better, or there will not be much left to worry over. Like St. Sophia, the buildings will stand, but the original spirit and intention will be gone. Something else will take their places.

In many ways things went too well, too long, for educational institutions. Fired by the coals of an expanding economy and riding the crest of public awe, the system of higher education sailed on. Voices of criticism were drowned in a chorus of "full steam ahead." It is difficult to preach to those who are enjoying an exhilarating ride. Now things have changed. We are running low on steam. Worse yet, the rudder is missing. The winds and waves are real, and they will not go away.

Our first order of business is to accept current circumstances, to take advantage of whatever we can, to seize this opportunity to reevaluate our condition, to establish priorities, to rededicate ourselves to the principles and purposes of the institution. But, what is the primary purpose of a university, in particular, of Washington State University? I am going to give an answer, but first, let us clear the air and list a few, some very much cherished, activities that are *not* primary purposes.

A primary purpose of a university is not to prepare students for a good job, not to grant degrees, not to obtain grants from the federal government, not to be an instrument of social justice, not to compete with community colleges and state colleges for the "student pool," not to screen candidates for professional schools, not to provide a hostel for prolonging adolescence, not to conform to the whims of a fickle public, not to field athletic teams, not to provide a haven for the unprepared, the indolent, and the irresponsible. The list goes on.

Many of you gasp. Why, one of these purposes is exactly the reason I am here. Certainly, individuals come to the university for a myriad of reasons; some acceptable, some not. Yet, no single one of these could possibly stand as a primary purpose of a university. Then, what *is* the purpose of a university?

The purpose of the university is to provide the resources and environment where the pursuit of knowledge, the exercise of criticism, and the performance of research can occur in a creative atmosphere of dedication, and the fruits of these endeavors, both methodology and results, can be transmitted to the society and posterity through instruction and publication. In a few words, the purpose is the pursuit of academic excellence by all concerned—faculty, students, administration, and staff.

With this fundamental statement let us now contrast a few of the facts, current activities, and documented trends of the last few years. (a) Standards of achievement in basic skills of the incoming students have fallen. I have personally documented this trend at WSU in the physical sciences and mathematics, and it has finally been revealed as a national phenomenon both in these areas and in others as well. At WSU the average arithmetic ability of new students has fallen 15 percent in five years. Does this sound like a student body that is prepared for the pursuit of excellence? (b) The study of foreign languages in colleges and universities is on the decline. The almost universal reaction is to drop the requirement. This does not sound like the pursuit of knowledge to me. It sounds more like capitulation to mediocrity. (c) A substantial fraction of the incoming students cannot read with comprehension and cannot write coherently. They obviously have access to the university, but can they really benefit from attendance? (d) We have all succumbed to the disease of vocabulary inflation. Let me illustrate. We say athletic scholarship; we mean athletic subsidy. We say needs scholarship; we mean educational subvention. We say that the student has difficulty with math; we mean he cannot do eighth grade arithmetic. We say that the student has difficulty expressing himself on paper; we mean he cannot write. The student is motivationally disadvantaged; the student is lazy. (e) We have grade inflation. While the achievement levels go down, the gpa (grade point average) goes up. A+ is really B; B is really C−; C is really

D —; D means the student attended for at least half the semester; F means the student forgot to complete the paperwork to withdraw.

The charade goes on. If the trend continues, soon we will have most of the graduating class at this banquet. Then we will have created the ultimate in academic irony, an Honor Society without honor.

I could go on, but it is really unnecessary to do so. Most of you in this room know something is wrong. After all, the scandal of falling standards reached the pages of *Newsweek* and has finally received the supreme accolade of academic respectability. In *Harper's Magazine* we read that it is happening at Harvard, too.

Our confusion is so deep seated that we no longer understand the meaning of simple words and phrases. The pursuit of excellence is equated with espousal of elitism; the compilation of credits is deemed an education; the mission of the university is confused with that of a community college; the obtaining of a grant is confused with scholarship; research is equated with money. The use of gimmicks is equated with good teaching. Quality is quantity. Bigger is better. Obscurity is profundity.

How disoriented we are is illustrated in the recent pages of our student newspaper, the *Daily Evergreen*. Two of my distinguished collegues felt compelled to defend research at this institution. The appalling aspect of all this is that any defense of research should be required! The battle against ignorance and confusion is becoming a desperate one.

Our confusion of quality with quantity is well illustrated in current efforts by virtually every committee on campus to develop a method for measuring teaching effectiveness. Teaching is a human activity and cannot be reduced entirely to numbers. Some judgments must be subjective. Attempting to reduce all to a statistical compilation of "Does the professor use slides? Does the teacher write distinctly on the board? Are the lectures delivered with clear diction?" will always be an exercise in futility. Even a lecturer who stutters, wears mismatched clothes, writes illegibly, and forgets to make assignments will pack them in if he or she is fair, exudes enthusiasm, commands respect, and demands excellence. No one will really give a damn if no slides are used. The students will recognize an example of committed integrity, even if they cannot define it, measure it, or spell it. And they will love it. They will also acquire something of value, something that is not measured on exams but is the foundation of a lifelong adventure of the mind. In short, some of them will acquire an education. Nonetheless, the futile search for a truly objective numerical measure of teaching effectiveness will continue. Even in science, however, some judgments are subjective.

Criticism is easy. Armchair coaching is a favorite sport. Ask our basketball coach. I suspect he has heard plenty of it. But criticism is not enough. We must have action. Where do we look for leadership? To whom do we turn to help us weather the storms, restore our confidence, make us focus on the real issues, and give us the strength to ignore those that dissipate our energies without benefiting our lot? Can we look to society? How can we, when the university is the capstone of the educational structure? Almost by definition the leadership of higher education must come from higher education. Should we look to other institutions? Should we appeal to Berkeley, to Illinois, to Harvard for leadership? My answer is a resounding "No!" Too many institutions have blindly followed the path of a few excellent ones (subjectively evaluated, I might add), and now they find themselves in similar uncomfortable circumstances. The answer to our search for leadership is a simple one. Look within for leadership and develop our own course of action. Evaluate current activities and establish priorities based on the fundamental premises of our existence. Discard that which saps energy and resources without promoting the primary purposes of the university.

Well, that is pretty vague. Let us be specific. Here are a few recommendations:

To the faculty: Reassert hegemony over course content. Delete the trivial and consolidate on principles. Introduce the relevant only when it serves to promote excellence in instruction and scholarship. Reassert the fundamental importance of research and scholarship as primary activities of the professoriate. Demand competence in the classroom. Throw away the "curve." Publicize clearly and well what will be demanded and stick to it. Insist on standards. Stop espousing the current invertebrate psychology that leads to condoning late withdrawals, raising grades under pressure, giving make-up exams, and preventing testing before vacations. Demand an improvement in the quality of incoming students. If the high school gpa is no longer a reliable index of achievement in basic skills (and there are very good reasons to suspect this), then demand competence examinations for entrance. Stop coddling the unmotivated, the poorly prepared, the chiselers, and the whiners. Flunk them. They do not deserve to be here. Your time is too valuable to waste on them. It is also too expensive, as the society is beginning to find out! Focus your attention on those who have prepared to attend the university, who have not wasted their high school years, who not only desire access to higher education but who are prepared to profit from it. Too long have we ignored our best. The nation cannot long survive such practices. Be proud to be a teacher, a scholar, a researcher. Be an example of committed integrity to your students. Teaching in a modern major university is a demanding profession; it is also a noble one. You have something important to say; say it with conviction, and say it with pride.

To the students: Demand excellence in the classroom, not only of your teachers, but of yourselves. If you want to be coddled, go back to high school; if you want to dissipate yourselves, go elsewhere; if you are not mature enough to profit from attendance at a university, try a community college or go look for a job. It will be better for you, and for society. Later on, when you are mature, maybe you can come back. Analyze your reasons for attending. Are you really interested in an education? Do you really want to exercise your mind? Or are you only interested in the path of least resistance, the accumulation of minimal credits, to obtain a minimal degree, to land a minimal comfortable job? If the latter is true, transfer to a vocational school. The state has provided them for you. They are just what you need. Actively seek an education. Do not stop at the minimum. Minimal requirements are just that—minimal requirements. Education can be a lifelong process. It is a great adventure. It does not consist of 120 credits and a diploma.

It is clear that I am talking to the wrong people. This is a habit of mine. Students in this room have risen to the top. That is why they are here. Now I ask you. What really happened at WSU? Did you experience long hours of boredom while the professor laboriously explained something to others that you understand and mastered in high school? Did you walk out early on any exams, because you finished long before the period ended? Did you find a course paced so slowly that attendance for only half the time was sufficient to ensure an A or B? Did you sprinkle a few "Mickey Mouse" offerings into the schedule to keep up the old grade point? Did you sign up pass/fail for a necessary course because you thought it was going to be a tough one? What about W's? Did you ever withdraw from a course because you thought you were headed for a C? If the answer is "yes" to any of these, then you were cheated at WSU. Either the institution cheated you, or you cheated yourself.

I look out and see that no one has shouted "yes." What a sterling group! I congratulate the officers for being so perceptive in their selections.

Seriously, though, we really do have a problem. The university has become so inundated with unprepared people, unmotivated people, confused people that we are having difficulty finding the real students, those who not only desire access to the university but have also prepared themselves to profit from attendance. You see, I did it here tonight. I spent my time (and your time) discussing those who really should not be at WSU, whereas I should have spent my time talking about what the university should be doing for you, for those who really care about scholarship and the pursuit of excellence.

Good students, prepared students, motivated students still come to the university. Oh, yes, they are here. You are the proof. Our problem is to find you quickly and having found you, make sure that you profit maximally from being here. The question is: How can we do it? Well, here are a few suggestions:

(a) Establish entrance examinations for WSU. What kind? Reading comprehension, writing ability, arithmetical skills, logical thinking. Now, I am not talking about high standards. I just want to make certain that freshmen can read and write well enough to understand college textbooks, comprehend lectures, and express themselves on paper, even if only in a mimimal way. How else can they profit from being here?

(b) Eliminate all remedial material from college courses. If students are deficient, set up autotutorial sequences for them to go through and obtain competence. [Ideally, the need for these should eventually vanish.] (c) Block enrollment of students in courses for which they are not prepared. Allow them to enroll only after they have demonstrated competence in prerequisites. (d) Emphasize and encourage the use of advanced standing examinations to allow the truly motivated and prepared to enter advanced courses with deliberate speed so that they can realize their full potential.

(e) Raise the General University Requirements both by number of courses and by quality of the offerings, *especially* the quality of the offerings. (f) Raise the minimal requirements for academic probation. (g) Trim the curriculum of

those special offerings that are designed for a certain clien-
tele but end up becoming an escape route for those who
just want to satisfy credit requirements rather than to
learn anything. (h) Restore the C as a respectable grade.
(i) Restore foreign language study to its proper place
in the curriculum. (j) Examine the entire curriculum, department by department, degree by degree, and weed out
the shoddy, the trivial, the intellectually flabby.

In short, we should look at each practice, procedure,
course, requirement, etc., and ask the questions, "Does this
really conform to the primary purpose of the institution?
Is it really in the spirit of the pursuit of excellence?"

Think what would happen in a few short years if such
a plan were implemented, even partially. Student and
faculty morale would improve. A new spirit of adventure
and scholarship would permeate the campus. Scholarship
and research would receive the homage they deserve and
real education would begin to be promoted. Confidence
would be restored, and our pride would return.

What kind of graduates would such an institution produce? Would they drift away in apathy and toss the alumni
support requests into the waste can, or would they constitute a new breed? I suspect that a dedicated core of them
would decide to support academic excellence. Rest assured;
support for athletics would continue. There are plenty of
champions for that cause. What about scholarship, however?
Is it possible that we could produce a group of alumni who
cared enough about academic excellence to endow a chair?
Think of it, a group of students, former students, and
friends who understood the real needs of the university
well enough to provide it with one or more prestigious
professorships. What a monument that would be! It would
signal to the state and to the nation that WSU's graduates
really obtained an education along with their degrees. It is
really too heady to contemplate.

The Cathedral of St. Sophia became a museum. People
still frequent her halls and chambers, but more to satisfy

curiosity than historical interest, and certainly not for religious edification. Decades from now WSU will still stand. A flight over the Palouse hills will reveal her walls gleaming in the sunlight. Will she have realized her potential as a university, or will she be a hollow mockery? The hour of decision is at hand and you, her faculty, illustrious students and eventual alumni must help her make the right choice. Help her make use of adversity.

"FAITH THAT ENLIVENS THE MIND" [7]

Krister Stendahl [8]

On January 8, 1977, Lenoir-Rhyne College, a Lutheran school at Hickory, North Carolina, inaugurated Dr. Albert B. Anderson as its eighth president. More than seventy-five representatives of colleges, universities, the Lutheran churches, and other organizations joined in the ceremonies. At 10:30 A.M. in the P. E. Monroe Auditorium on the campus, Dr. Krister Stendahl, dean of the Harvard University Divinity School, delivered the inaugural address, based upon a text from Romans 12:2, "Do not be conformed to this age, but rather be transformed by the renewal of your mind."

The speech was intended to inspire newly installed President Anderson, the board of trustees, and members of the college community, but it holds meaning for almost any denominational college audience in the United States. In developing his theme, "The faith that enlivens the mind is the faith that a college needs," Dean Stendahl strives to articulate the guiding principle of a privately supported church college that professes to offer a *Christian* education, an education different from what is to be found in other academic institutions. But a thoughtful reading suggests that it is also a statement for what any excellent liberal arts institution might strive for, that is, the molding of attitudes.

The speaker amplifies his theme through the citation of five additional references from scripture as well as by emphasizing his text through repetition (over ten times). His presentation is deceivingly simple, building toward the final sentence, "Seek ye first the kingdom of God and all the rest will come somehow." The choice of words, sentence structure, and simple style are indicative of the oral mode, suggesting perhaps that the text might have been transcribed from a recording.

Dear Al et al, or as Paul said in the Epistle, dear brothers and sisters. He didn't, but he would if he were here now.

I have chosen to reflect on this important and delightful

[7] Delivered at Lenoir-Rhyne College, Hickory, North Carolina, January 8, 1977. The speech was first published in *Profile, Lenoir-Rhyne Magazine*, February 1977, p 7-8. Quoted by permission.
[8] For biographical note, see Appendix.

occasion on those well-known words in the twelfth chapter of Paul's epistle to the Romans. And the phrase that has caught my imagination specifically is, of course, the one which says in various translations something like, "Do not be conformed to this age, but rather be transformed by the renewal of your mind." Or if I were to paraphrase, I would say that verse reads something like, "Do not fall for the fads of your generation, rather let your perspective become changed by the renewal of your mind so that you can see what God wants, what is good, and delightful, and bears the mark of the Kingdom of God."

The faith that enlivens the mind is the faith that a college needs. And if it is a church-related college, then that college has to demand of the church that it supplies intensively and freely out of the treasure of faith, *that* faith which enlivens the mind. Not the one which stifles it. Because there have been examples in the history of education and in the history of the church of faiths so conceived and so expressed that they actually stifle the mind. And that is because the spirit and the faith has often been used by us human beings in selfish manners. Actually, that is the sin of sins according to good Lutheran theology, that we use God's gifts and even the revelation and the Ten Commandments to our own security and gain.

When the frustrated parent shouts to the kid, "Honor your father and your mother," it is a little hard for the kid to hear the unpolluted word of God, because it seems that that is quoted in a situation so obviously to advantage to the older set. And when the truly, truly hungry mother has taken a loaf of bread to feed her child, and rich and well-fed society shouts, "Thou shalt not steal," that is right and that is a quote from the scriptures and even the Ten Commandments, but, it's obvious that we use the law for our selfish protection.

And the faith committed to the saints and the spirit shed abroad has often been used by us scared and uptight Christians in selfish manner for security and safety rather than for exploration. But according to the scriptures, both the faith and the spirit are primarily for those who have the urge and the courage to venture into the unknown, into the uncharted places of the earth and of the mind and of the imagination. And who is, according to the Bible, the Father of faith? His name was Abraham. And he, as it says in Hebrews, and as it is witnessed to in the Old Testament, he was the one who went out from that which was known and the traditions of his ancestors, not knowing where he was to go. And that is and remains the true sign of the truly religious person, he or she just doesn't know where to go, but he or she has enough trust in God to set out even so. And so also in the travels of the mind, and that's why the faith enlivens the mind.

Or think of the spirit, that creative wind of God that brooded over the chaos waters, filling matter with life. But so much life and so much freedom and so much enlivening, that already in Genesis chapter 3, the Fall occurs. God chose freedom, knowing the risk. And it is in God's wisdom that the Lord rather somehow, as also is so clear from the life and style of Jesus, prefers enlivened sinners to dead dullness. Think of the spirit that enlivens with risk.

And so, my sisters and my brothers, we have gathered here to pray God that that endeavoring faith and that enlivening spirit will fill the mind and the will and the imagination and the inventiveness of Albert Anderson and this college during his presidency.

This is a church college, although faculty often prefer to call it a private college, and some others, too. And there has been much discussion about the place and the role of these church colleges. And all of us here have been involved in one way or another in such conversations or reflections. And the pros and cons have been weighed. I think there can be no doubt that the time is right for a more distinctive style, lifestyle and educational style, of churches conscious of their being part of the church's mission. There was a time when this was debatable. But the process of sameness has gone far enough. And the experiment with a boldness of faith certainly has its place.

Now, the reasons for church colleges have suffered much erosion. Often one finds, especially if one dusts off some of the phrases and really tries to find what is said, that the greatest chance of church colleges to attract students is that parents who pay for the education find church colleges a little safer—safer in terms of sex and sometimes safer even in terms of the mind. That strikes me as not quite sufficient a base nor a good one for the perpetuation of places like this.

Another rather delightful aspect of the argument for these colleges is that they are small, humane and have a very attractive student/faculty ratio. And that is very nice and very important. But it is also a sign of American affluence which one wonders how long the world will be able to sustain. It is an enormously expensive luxury that most of the world will never be able to afford. And as long as the church colleges are living out of the satisfaction and filling in the gap when, so they say, the world can't afford that kind of education anymore, the nice church people can still sort of hang in there and afford it, there is no future. Because this is an economic question.

It's almost the same that has happened in many countries where the churches have hospitals. These were genuinely Samaritan missions into the world one hundred fifty years ago. But now in many parts of Europe and in some parts of this country, the church-related hospitals are the ones where you can buy extra friendly care with a Christian shiver in the hand of the nurse as she puts it on your feverish forehead—if you can afford it. It has become the luxury form of care, and we have to guard ourselves carefully lest the church-related college becomes the luxury type of higher education.

There must be other and better reasons. And the reason above reasons, as I see it, is that in a pluralistic world, we will be set free to be more distinct in our own little "we,"

the value and the glory and the necessity of distinct ways
of variety and of clear witness. The pendulum is no doubt
swinging, beginning to swing back, from seeing it as if the
problem of the church-related college was to just be a college that happens to have church support. It is in the educational center that the question has to be raised.

Thus the real problem about the church-related college
is not whether it should be related to the church or not, but
what faith and what spirit gives shape to that relationship.
The test is this: Is the college a place where the faith enlivens the mind? Is the college in the tradition of Abraham, the father of the faith, who went toward the unknown
rather than cultivating the faith of his past? Is the college
in its relation to the church sustained by the spirit of creation, with freedom and risk and forgiveness and redemp-
tion?

Thus, to the church the college is a great challenge. Its
role within the totality of the church is sort of prophetic.
And heaven knows that one of the unsafest things to invest
in in the world is to invest in prophets, because their job is
to keep you honest, and to push on under the spirit. The
college's role is sort of prophetic. It is not an agent toward
security or self-preservation. It's the laboratory of the future. It is the constant and ever-renewed roll call of faith
from Hebrews 11: "In faith they went out, in faith they held
out, God not being behind them, but in our future." That
is the charisma of the gift of the college. And this gift of
the college is to have a strong share, a strong portion, in
the faith of the church. And the way to measure how much
faith there is is to measure whether the minds are enlivened.
The more enlivened mind is a sign of a richer faith.

And so as we gather here with the Board of Trustees
and all, one word comes easily to one's mind. And that is
the word *endowment*. That's a big word and will be very
important to President Anderson, to not only meditate
upon but to do and make. For today we ask for *the* endow-

ment, *the* endowment of the spirit that enlivens the mind. No other way of faith or spirit is good enough for Lenoir-Rhyne college. For as Jesus said, "Seek ye first the kingdom of God, and all the rest will come somehow." Amen.

LANGUAGE AND THE LIVED WORLD [9]

WALLACE A. BACON [10]

On April 8, at 10:30 A.M., Professor Wallace A. Bacon, president of the Speech Communication Association, addressed the General Session of the annual convention of the Southern Speech Communication Association at the Hyatt Regency Hotel, Knoxville, Tennessee. He spoke to an audience of about 150 teachers and administrators from the southern states.

In his carefully prepared speech Professor Bacon, who teaches the interpretation of literature in the School of Speech at Northwestern University, reminded his listeners of the importance of appreciating the nuances of the language of poetry, drama, and public address, or in his words, "the relation between language and the lived world."

To his immediate audience of teachers of speech communication and to readers, actors, and speakers, he suggests another way of making some useful distinctions among the "varying relationships with language." Instead of focusing upon it as a practical means of reaching listeners, he thinks of language "as a way of getting the feeling of the lived world into the process of thought about the world." He prefers words that embrace the wonderment of childhood and the intensity of the poet. He wants delivered language, "not tied simply to perception," but employed to elicit dreaming, remembering, imagining, and thinking.

Professor Bacon, teacher, reader, lecturer, and critic, is an effective communicator. Through his diction, and his voice control, and his platform demeanor, he gives full meaning to his message. When he utters his well-chosen words, he becomes almost a poet, demonstrating through delivery what he says in his speech.

At a time when so much effort goes into striving and selling, Bacon asks us to search for the richness that well-delivered language may communicate. His love for literature with its power to exalt offers a contrast to the word manipulation of the hard sell in slogans and fifteen-second TV spots. He points up the satisfaction in working with "one of the most marvelous of all instru-

---

[9] Delivered at 10:30 A.M., April 18, 1977, at the general session of the annual convention of the Southern Speech Communication Association, Grand Ballroom, Hyatt Regency Hotel, Knoxville, Tennessee. Quoted by permission.

[10] For biographical note, see Appendix.

ments, the language of human beings" and says "We can lose ourselves in it. We can find ourselves."

Whatever is to be said—and much is to be said—for the importance of nonverbal and visual forms of communication, the fact remains that it is the use of language which strikes most of us as being at the heart of interactions between human beings. And for our discipline, it is language as psychological speech act which gives us a focus, which binds us together as students and as scholars, which permits us to function with our fellows in human society.

In a review of a new volume by James Edie (to appear in I think the next issue of *The Quarterly Journal of Speech*), I suggested that it may be our varying relationships with language which distinguish some branches of Speech Communication from others. Traditionally, we have talked of those differences as arising from relationships with audiences—the speaker accepts direct address to an audience as his realm; the interpreter moves between direct and indirect appeals to an audience; the actor's relationship is indirect. But as dramatic texts become more open, as interpreters move closer to actors and actors to interpreters, as the speaker's address varies from explicit persuasion to (say) eulogy or personal memory, these distinctions become difficult to sustain and often seem not worth mentioning.

Edie's volume—without, I think, intending deliberately anything like the distinction I am going to make—suggested to me another way of making some useful distinctions. And I must go back beyond his beginning point in order to make them. The language of childhood often seems to students of literature a kind of forsaken ideal. If we could all keep that miraculous sense of the poetic which children have, they say. How imaginative is their use of language! The little girl who first saw a lamb and felt of it and said wonderingly, "It's all made of blankets"—how marvelously expressive that is of the lamb's wool. And what a striking conjunction of lamb and bedcover.

It's true enough that children talk this way—and it's true enough that it is wonderful to us. Children learn the lived world by metaphor—the tiger is a big kitty. For a time, one kitty is all kittens; then kittens become distinct; and tigers become distinct from cats. The mind both separates and categorizes kinds; things no longer exist miraculously linked in metaphor but become real "facts." We may say of a lamb that its wool *feels like* a blanket, but we are not likely, even as *young* adults, to say that the lamb is all made of blankets.

There is no use wishing that we could stop at that childlike sense of the world (which we think of as wonder). It would not do to have Jimmy Carter say of his blanket, "It's all made of lambs," though we may accept from him certain other childlike things said without metaphor. No, as adults, we are asked to say what we mean, to mean what we say, and to have a clear grasp of the external world, however foggy we may be about the worlds within.

For adults, in the process of thinking, language moves us away from the world of lived experience. That is inevitable. It isn't a question of good or bad, but a matter of fact. An awareness of the body in the lived world is subordinated to the processes of thought. If we were aware of every bodily sensation accompanying every thought as we tried to answer questions, tried to persuade, tried to express our feelings, we would probably become tongue-tied; we would certainly seem odd to our listeners.

I am not, of course, suggesting that the body disappears when we think, nor that we are totally unaware of it. But in the context of thinking, bodily awareness is not (when we are at our best) uppermost with us. That seems to me as it should be. That, it seems to me, is the situation of the speaker in the context of traditional rhetoric.

But for the actor and interpreter, the relationship between language and the lived world is clearly different. A play or a poem or a story by and large wants to embody *both* the processes of thought and the processes of lived experience in the body. Sometimes such language is said to be self-referencing. It calls attention to itself as a way of saying even while it is saying. It makes use of metaphor as a radical vehicle of meaning. When Wordsworth wants to convey the notion that once earlier in his life the objects of the world had a sense of wonder attached to them, he says:

> There was a time when meadow, grove, and stream,
> The earth, and every common sight,
>> To me did seem
>> Apparelled in celestial light,
> The glory and the freshness of a dream.

He specifies—meadow, grove, and stream, common sights all —but probably a reader begins to see not simply general groves and meadows and streams but particular ones drawn from his or her memory. And they are "clothed"—apparelled; and in something heavenly, a celestial light. They may have the unreality of a dream, but they have the glory and the freshness of a dream. Or had. To the literal-minded, this is all just flowers, purple passages. To the poet, it is a way of getting the feel of the lived world into the process of thought about that world. Rhyme and the use of inverted syntax contribute to his effects.

The poet may achieve this "feel" by prosodic means— breaking up the natural flow of thought and intensifying sensations. William Carlos Williams wants to say, "I have eaten the plums that were in the icebox and which you were probably saving for breakfast. Forgive me; they were delicious; so sweet and so cold." That is a very clear statement, perhaps the husband to his wife: "Sorry, my dear; I ate those plums you wanted to save for our breakfast, and I'm sorry, but they were really good." That is a thought— or two or three thoughts. And it has some expression of feeling: I'm sorry. But what happens if you do as Williams does, and strengthen the pressure of those simple words practically to the breaking point:

I have eaten
the plums
that were in
the icebox

and which
you were probably
saving
for breakfast.

Forgive me
they were delicious,
so sweet
and so cold.[11]

One can capture a sense of amusement, a mock apology (though a felt one), a sharing of complicity in the event of eating the plums, so that the meaning becomes an experience, put back into the lived world where it happened. Taste the plums. See the icebox. What else is for breakfast? It is not *something* which *somebody* did, but *a* thing which *a* person did, feelingly.

In this view, perhaps philosophical thought (like scientific thought) stands at one end of the continuum. Personal essays stand somewhere near the middle. The lyric statement stands at the other end. Language does not want always to capture the lived world; one of its glories, as a vehicle for human interaction, is that it can free us from the lived world. We are not tied simply to perception of what it is. We can dream, we can remember, we can imagine. We can *think*.

But the poet and the playwright, in varying degrees in varying pieces, value the tie between thought and the lived world. They live on it. They can in fact create experience through it. The experience of the poem becomes now a part of our experience of the lived world—the poem lives in the

[11] "This Is Just to Say" from William Carlos Williams' *Collected Earlier Poems*, copyright © 1938 by the author and published by New Directions Corporation. Reprinted by permission.

world, and it changes our lives. Far from wanting to transcend the lived world, we now want to glory in it—not at the *expense* of thought, but as a way of intensifying the *feeling* of thought. Now we *do* want to be aware, as fully aware as possible, of the motions of our bodies as we think.

There are always boorish people who find the speaker dull and the actor engaging, or the actor dull and the speaker significant. Speakers have *something to say*, they will put it. Actors only *love to hear the sounds of their own voices*. Or (conversely) speakers *talk talk talk*; actors *entertain*. What a silly world they live in, those people who will find pleasure in rhetoric but hate literature; or who talk about "mere rhetoric" and wallow in the delights of the soap opera. Grownups inhabit both worlds, or ought to. What good is a parent who has no sense of what the world is like to a child? How sad that that child, grown parent, forgets the metaphorical world in which he grew. Not that the child can remain child—who wants that? But what is the point in losing that wonderful world where most of us grew up and which has brought so much to wherever we may be now?

You can see that I have a professional bias on the side of the poet and the child—but not because the speaker and rhetoric seem to me less significant. I value what rhetoric has taught me about literature and about criticism. I value what the communication theorist is teaching me about language, about interaction among human beings. I value the immediacy of the real world seen on television and the imaginary world seen often in film. I can listen to Alistair Cooke (that excellent *teacher*) as he talks to me about "Upstairs-Downstairs" (though I am not much instructed by John Gielgud as he reads to me about "The Pallisers"), and then I move into the lived world of the Bellamys and Hudson and Mrs. Bridges and Rose and Ruby and Edward and all the rest of those fascinating humans who have now become a part of my own life. I *see* them; they are literally objects of perception for me. When I move to poems, I no longer have Wordsworth's tree or meadow or grove there to perceive literally, but I must perceive them imaginatively, and Wordsworth's language in its miraculous way permits me to do that. The poet creates; when I move through the felt sensing of his poem, I, too, create. Not just thoughts, worlds—worlds which become part of my lived experience.

As teachers and students of speech communication, we work with one of the most marvelous of all instruments: the language of human beings. We can lose ourselves in it. We can find ourselves in it. I don't know about you, but I cannot imagine a more humanly satisfying occupation than the one we daily share, in our exploration of the relationships between people and the worlds they live in by way of the most human of channels: speech.

FOR FREEDOM'S BIRTHDAY

THE TALL SHIPS [1]

Francis B. Sayre Jr. [2]

Of all the events of the Bicentennial, nothing stirred the imagination of Americans more than the coming of the tall ships, high-masted square-riggers carrying enormous expanse of sail. They came from Russia, Japan, Poland, Great Britain, Italy, East Germany, Argentina, Chile, and several regions of the United States, these full-masted vessels reminiscent of John Masefield's affecting line, "And all I ask is a tall ship and a star to steer her by" ("Sea Fever").

The ships assembled at Bermuda and raced northward, arriving at Newport, Rhode Island, June 26, 1976, in spite of inept crews, three collisions, and a "mammoth calm" en route. In full sail but under the power of their motors, the great ships paraded into the harbor on June 27, gave the spectators a thrill "at the sight of the young cadets standing high on the ship's superstructure (Libertad of Argentina), a maneuver known as 'dressing the yard'" (John Kifner, New York *Times*, June 27, 1976). Estimates were that 90,000 to 95,000 spectators packed the waterfront to enjoy the carnival atmosphere and mix "with smartly dressed cadets from many nations" (Jak Miner, *Christian Science Monitor*, June 28, 1976).

On any occasion the spectacle of sailing ships is likely to arouse imaginations and bring forth eloquence. The Very Reverend Francis B. Sayre Jr., dean of Washington Cathedral, delivered a Bicentennial Sermon on Sunday, June 27, 1976, at Trinity Church at Newport. This superb, short speech gains its motive power from the minister's apt analogies between the sailing vessels and the lives of his listeners. He is most skillful at filling his discourse with numerous references to ships and the sea. Persons who heard the exhortation must have been caught up in its vitality.

"Steady as you go"—on tossing sea or smooth, that ancient order to the helm links generation after generation of

---

[1] Delivered as a Bicentennial sermon at Trinity Church, Newport, Rhode Island, June 27, 1976. Quoted by permission.

[2] For biographical note, see Appendix.

seafarers, keeping to their course upon the deep, pitting their purpose against the primeval power of wind and wave and unseen current.

"Keep your stem to the heading: leave a straight wake astern!" That would have been John Cabot's instruction to his quartermaster in the tiny ship Mathew in the year 1497 as he made for what he thought would turn out to be the oriental Isles of Spice, only to find that he and his eighteen men had arrived, fifty-two days out of Bristol, on the foggy coast of Labrador.

A century later navigators knew a little more about geography, enough so that the little Golden Hind could make it round the world in two years, four months. Think of the patient courage of Francis Drake and his men who survived those watery years, and in the long midwatch ever bade the steersmen, "Steady as you go!"

Steady course, steady purpose! Have they not ever been married upon the sea?

Vessel Mayflower, 180 tons burden, setting sail in 1620 from Old England, in quest of a New, the eyes of all one hundred passengers bent firmly upon the West, where God might make a fresh beginning with them, and they with God.

Constitution, Constellation, Flying Cloud, ships of war and ships of peace, whalers and clippers and coast-wise schooners; they bred all of them a sturdy race, looking to the stars by night and the horizon by day for those unswerving signs by which a mariner is guided: by which he may discern that same Father of Lights of whom the Bible speaks, "with whom is no variableness, neither shadow of turning."

Thus are we grateful, on this Sunday of national remembrance, to all these captains and their crews who have sailed across the rolling main, and come at last to this ancient port, to remind us of our youth and to refresh our hope. They man a fleet of beautiful and stately grace, built like ships before them of the skill of careful artisans; and sailed by courage in the tops, and discipline upon the deck below, by those who have striven to embody the plain and precious blessings with which this continent came to be endowed.

Their word to us this morning, and to all of America, is simply that the landfall is the same as it was two hundred years ago. The course is constant: the goal unchanged. "Steady as you go."

So should a nation's purpose be: fixed and clear. To build in the great shipyard of this land a vessel for all of us, tall enough to go anywhere and everywhere the spirit might ordain, yet so stoutly fastened in her every timber—ribs to keel, knees to ribs, planking on top and masts stepped in between—that no storm should breach her hull or undo her patient plan.

Such a ship, hewn in responsibility, but with freedom at her prow, was the little bark that was launched to independence two centuries ago. And other men on other shores watched the pennants atop her spars, to see which way she would fly, or whether it was all just a dream. How many since then have followed in her train!—as now this Bicentennial fleet from their several coasts across the sea.

But these sailors also know, what some citizens have forgot in this latter day: that no purpose is achieved, nor any course made good upon God's ocean, until first you have trimmed your sails and set the helm to fit *His* winds and the set of *His* tide upon the deep.

Keen is the mariner's eye to discern those telling signs upon the clouds, at the line 'twixt sky and water, or on the crest of waves where the spindrift blows, by which he might foretell the bluster or the calm, the weather God has in store for him.

And if he is so fortunate as to find a wind that blows from Heaven exactly in the direction he would go on earth, then easy and gay the skipper who can barrel down before that wind, all canvas set, rolling along upon the bosom of the blast.

This has been America in these latter times; affluent and easy, not having to work very hard to run out her log; just cruising wing and wing, tide and breeze at her back, and the men lolling upon the deck, a beer in their hand.

But more often in this world it is a head wind that we face—then, though the bearing of your destination be precisely the same, you have to tack—back and forth, back and forth; close-hauled; wind in your face, spray on your legs; fingers white upon the sheet, body tensed against the bucking tiller; fine-tuning your lively lady to the majestic forces of splendid Creation; and so wresting from that opposing wind the destiny of your desire.

That's when your boat must needs be staunch and true, well braced and put together, and lithe like a living thing. And that is when the sailor too is on his mettle, no less in command for all his reverence in the presence of a power mightier than his own.

This also I take to be the message of these tall ships, coming here on freedom's birthday: their voyage is made to demonstrate that liberty is not the toy of whim, not mere indulgence of each sailor's dream, or any citizen's selfish wish; but rather is founded upon a deeper consonance with those eternal laws which God ordained to rule the universe: laws of brotherhood, laws of truth, laws of love and sacrifice and the humble integrity of self-discipline. You go by *His* wind for these are the laws "whose service is perfect freedom."

Let us remember that they are given by that "Father of Lights, with whom is no variableness, neither shadow of turning," that same God whose Word to us in the centuries ahead can be naught else but simply and quietly: "Steady as you go."

BICENTENNIAL OF AMERICAN INDEPENDENCE [3]

WARREN E. BURGER, CARL ALBERT,
NELSON A. ROCKEFELLER, AND GERALD R. FORD [4]

The Bicentennial commemoration, spread out over two years, opened with the reenactment of the First Continental Congress at Carpenters' Hall, Philadelphia, September 5, 1974, and continued through 1976 with the restaging on Christmas night, 1976, of Washington's crossing of the Delaware. More than 8,000 communities across the country commissioned Bicentennial activities during 1975-1976. As a part of the Bicentennial Youth Debate program, students from over 8,500 high schools, colleges, and universities argued Revolutionary topics. Debates were staged between British and American students in Boston, Philadelphia, Los Angeles, and Springfield, Illinois (*Christian Science Monitor*, October 10, 1975). The National Broadcasting Company programmed 170 hours on Bicentennial themes, including an all-day report of how Americans spent July 4, 1976.

The activities climaxed during the week which included July 4, 1976. Around the nation, solemn gatherings, fireworks, parades, vigils (at Lincoln and Jefferson memorials, Washington, D.C.), and festivals were the order of the day. Mass naturalization services were conducted in Miami where 7,141 took the oath, and in Chicago (2,300) and Detroit (1,000). Communities competed for attention. The town of George, in Washington, claimed the largest cherry pie, sixty feet square; Baltimore had the largest cake—6,900 pounds. The fireworks display in the nation's capital consumed twenty-two tons of pyrotechnics. Thousands enjoyed the beaches, baseball games, and automobile races.

President Gerald Ford, Nelson Rockefeller and other prominent Americans gave epideictic speeches. The President spoke at the National Archives on July 2, 1976; at the John F. Kennedy Center for the Performing Arts, July 3; at Valley Forge State Park, Pennsylvania; in Independence Hall, Philadelphia; and, briefly, on board the USS Forrestal anchored in New York Harbor, where the tall ships passed in review.

Of course, much interest centered around the original manu-

---

[3] Delivered at approximately 9:00 P.M., July 2, 1976, at the National Archives, Washington, D.C. Quoted from *Weekly Compilation of Presidential Documents*, July 5, 1976, vol. 12, no. 12.

[4] For biographical notes, see Appendix.

script of the Declaration of Independence. During the seventy-six hours from Friday July 2 at 6 P.M. through Monday July 5 at 10:00 P.M. the National Archives put on continuous displays. The exhibit "Charters of Freedom" included the Declaration of Independence, the Constitution, and the Bill of Rights. The ceremonies were opened at 9:00 P.M., July 2, 1976, in Exhibition Hall at the National Archives with brief speeches from the leaders of four branches of the federal government (Washington *Post*, July 3, 1976).

Brief speeches were delivered by Chief Justice Warren Burger, representing the Supreme Court; Speaker Carl Albert, representing the House; Vice President Nelson Rockefeller as President of the Senate; and, of course, President Ford as Chief Executive. The Vice President presided and introduced each speaker, noting that they represented the three separate branches of our federal government. All the speeches took no more than thirty minutes. President Ford spoke for twelve.

The audience itself was a ceremonial one. Responding to an open invitation, 200 were standing in the Archives to view the ceremony, another 1,000 filled the stairs leading to the Constitution Avenue entrance of the Archives, and additional people stood on the sidewalk in front and across the street. Probably few of the audience in the Archives heard the speeches. Once the speeches were delivered the viewers began to file by the exhibit and to sign the register. It was a seventy-six-hour vigil. [Information supplied by James W. Mansfield, director of Media Services of the American Revolution Bicentennial Administration.]

Warren E. Burger

Thank you, Mr. Vice President. Mr. President, Mr. Speaker, distinguished guests, ladies and gentlemen:

The Declaration that is being honored tonight had no binding legal effect when it was announced two hundred years ago, but it guided the men who, eleven years later, drafted the Constitution.

The Declaration was a statement of intent and purpose. The Constitution was a compact of the people, a contract, if you will, to carry out the Declaration. Our Constitution created a government in which the people have the supreme and ultimate power. The opening words of the preamble tell us that we, the people, have agreed among ourselves that power must be used in an orderly way under rules laid down in the Constitution.

As schoolchildren, we learned that those who came to our shores agreed to give up some of their individual freedom for the common good. The Mayflower Compact and others like it were, in a sense, the forerunners of the Constitution, and that Constitution now stands as the greatest human compact in history.

Our form of government differs from all others ever devised. And ever since it was adopted, the Constitution has operated like the stars that guided the first travelers on the open seas where there were no landmarks to guide them.

Our Constitution is not perfect, and even less so are the mortals who must try to say what it means. But what is important is that it has been the guide to keep us on the paths of freedom that were laid out so long ago. The American people have firmly supported the Constitution and the means established to enforce its guarantees. It has been tested under the stress of internal and external warfare, by economic catastrophes and in political crises, and on every occasion the country has emerged stronger.

These two documents, the Declaration and the Constitution, embarked the American people on an experiment in a new form of government, self-government, that has survived longer than any other kind of government in recorded history. In this experiment, that remarkable group of American leaders wisely recognized the paradox of freedom: that to preserve liberty, each one of us must give some of it up.

This is why we have come to call our system one of ordered liberty, liberty exercised in an orderly way with restraints and with respect for the rights of others. To create and maintain such a system was the function of our Constitution.

The problems and burdens of those 3 million early Americans who began this experiment were so great from 1776 to 1789, that those leaders constantly called for divine guidance in their efforts. With the complexities of a nation now grown to 215 million people and the world problems that we must share, can we survive without it?

Washington, both as a general and as President, constantly called for divine guidance and credited all progress and success to that source. When the Declaration was signed, John Adams wrote his wife Abigail saying that "July 4 ought to be commemorated as the day of deliverance by solemn acts of devotion to Almighty God." And when the Constitution was finally approved, James Madison observed that "All people must perceive in the Constitution a finger of that Almighty hand which has been so frequently extended to our relief in the critical stages of the revolution."

We have survived and prospered for two hundred years now because the strength of our nation was not simply in the words of the Declaration or the Constitution, great as they are, but because of the strength of the people, of personal integrity, of individual responsibility, and of the tradition of home and family and of religious beliefs.

Our Constitution, no constitution, can solve all our problems. At its best, our Constitution gives the American people the means and the opportunity to find solutions—by their own efforts, by their dedication, and by their love of country.

The French historian de Tocqueville long ago wrote this about America:

I sought for the greatness and genius of America in her commodious harbors and her ample rivers, and it was not there; in her fertile fields and boundless prairies, and it was not there; in her rich gold mines and her vast world commerce, and it was not there. Not until I went into the churches of America did I understand the secret of her genius and her power. America is great because she is good and if America ever ceases to be good, America will cease to be great.

Carl Albert

Mr. President, Mr. Vice President, Mr. Chief Justice, distinguished guests, ladies and gentlemen:

The decisive act of separation from England actually took place on July 2, exactly two hundred years ago today, when the Continental Congress adopted the resolution of independence, drafted by a committee of five, headed by Thomas Jefferson. Thus, it is especially appropriate that we launch this Fourth of July weekend this evening, July 2.

On yesterday, the House of Representatives and the Senate unanimously passed Concurrent Resolution 672, wherein it was stated that "the Congress of the United States of America does hereby reaffirm its commitments to the ideals and principles expressed in the Declaration of Independence by members of the Congress assembled in Philadelphia on July 2, 1776."

The Declaration launched our quest for freedom. Five long years would pass before the English forces, led by General Cornwallis, would surrender at Yorktown. The emerging nation would struggle under ineffective Articles of Confederation for six more years, before formulating the Constitution in Philadelphia in 1787. The body of our Constitution set up our tripartite system of government and gave us a mechanism of government that would endure for generations and would enable us to accomplish our goals.

It was not until 1791, two years after the Constitution had been ratified, fifteen years after the signing of the Declaration of Independence, that the Bill of Rights breathed life into the immortal document known as the Declaration of Independence. It was handled in the Congress by James Madison, but it was the inspiration of the author of the Declaration of Independence.

The sage of Monticello wanted to make sure in his letters to many leading Americans in many states that the liberties which he proclaimed in 1776 would be given substance in the Constitution. Had it not been for that leadership, there would be no guaranteed freedom of worship, no freedom of speech, no freedom of press, no right of peaceful assemblage, no right to petition in case of grievances.

Because of the Bill of Rights to the Constitution, my

fellow Americans, no man may cross the threshold of your home without a search warrant, no man may cast you in prison without a trial by a jury of your peers. These are the concrete cornerstones of our liberty proclaimed in the Declaration of Independence; these are the basic principles of the ends of our system of government.

We meet tonight to rededicate ourselves to the perpetuation of these principles. To this end, it may be well to repeat the closing words of the Declaration of Independence itself: "With a firm Reliance on the Protection of divine Providence, we mutually pledge to each other our lives, our Fortunes, and our sacred Honor."

Nelson A. Rockefeller

In two hundred eventful years, we Americans have changed in every possible way, except in our fidelity to our fundamental political principles and institutions. Our republic remains the oldest, continuous, fundamentally unchanged political system in the world. Tonight, as we launch this Bicentennial weekend, let us remember, understand, and celebrate that remarkable fact.

We Americans remain the faithful political descendants of our Founding Fathers, because we continue to agree with the ideas they immortally expressed in the Declaration of Independence and the Constitution—the belief that liberty and democracy can be a blessing to mankind if carefully structured and moderated and, if not, a curse.

We Americans happily had a path marked out for us by the American Founders leading to the blessings of liberty and democracy.

We come here tonight to acknowledge our indebtedness to the principles and institutions they devised, to give witness to their success, and to renew our dedication to that compound and sober blend of liberty and democracy which is the essence of our national heritage. The very form of this ceremony tonight testifies to that compound and sober American blend of liberty and democracy.

We have here tonight the assemblage of the American democratic republic, a ceremony which celebrates, which assembles all of the representative elements of our two hundred-year-old political system.

Here in this Hall: the Chief Justice, the Speaker of the House of Representatives, and the President of the United States—representing our system of the separation of powers.

In my constitutional capacity as presiding officer of the Senate, I have the honor to represent the principle of bicameralism.

Here tonight also are governors and mayors and other local officials, representing the American principles of federalism and decentralization. And also joining in this assemblage of the republic are leaders of our private voluntary associations, representing the American principle of creative, private, voluntary action.

For all our faults and failings, we here tonight, gathered with all our fellow citizens everywhere, express the principles and represent the institutions devised by our Founding Fathers—separation of powers to protect liberty and also secure competent government power; bicameralism to balance and refine the popular will; federalism and decentralization to guard against despotism and to allow the American people energetically to solve their political problems as much as possible at the local level; and private, voluntary associations so that people themselves may freely and creatively supply their own needs without dependence upon paternal government.

Like our Founding Fathers, we do not believe in a simple centering of all power in a streamlined, monolith of government; rather, we believe that liberty and democracy can only be achieved by these complex principles and institutions of the American democratic republic.

We come back here tonight to draw strength anew from our old and tested principles and institutions, so that we may go forward with orderly creativity into our third century.

And now, ladies and gentlemen, it is my honor to present a man who, in two short years, has restored America's respect for our national leadership, has restored the vitality of our economy at home, and restored confidence in our leadership in the world—the President of the United States, Gerald R. Ford.

Gerald R. Ford

Thank you, Mr. Vice President, Mr. Speaker, Mr. Chief Justice, distinguished guests, ladies and gentlemen:

I am standing here before the great charters of American liberty under law. Millions of Americans, before me and after me, will have looked and lingered over these priceless documents that have guided our two hundred years of high adventure as "a new nation, conceived in liberty and dedicated to the proposition that all men are created equal."

Those were Lincoln's words as he looked to the Declaration of Independence for guidance when a raging storm obscured the Constitution. We are gathered here tonight to honor both.

Even the way these parchments are displayed is instructive—together, as they must be historically understood, the Constitution and its first ten amendments on an equal plane; the Declaration of Independence properly central and above all.

The Declaration is the Polaris of our political order—the fixed star of freedom. It is impervious to change, because it states moral truths that are eternal.

The Constitution provides for its own changes having equal force with the original articles. It began to change soon after it was ratified, when the Bill of Rights was added. We have since amended it sixteen times more, and before we celebrate our three hundredth birthday, there will be more changes.

But the Declaration will be there, exactly as it was when the Continental Congress adopted it—after eliminating and changing some of Jefferson's draft, much to his annoyance.

Jefferson's immortal words will remain, and they will be preserved in human hearts even if this original parchment should fall victim to time and fate.

Listen:

We hold these Truths to be self-evident, that all Men are created equal, that they are endowed by their Creator with certain unalienable Rights, that among these are Life, Liberty, and the Pursuit of Happiness—That to secure these Rights, Governments are instituted among Men, deriving their just Powers from the Consent of the Governed. . . .

The act of independence, the actual separation of colonies and Crown, took place two hundred years ago today, when the delegations of twelve colonies adopted Richard Henry Lee's resolution of independence. The founders expected that July 2 would be celebrated as the national holiday of the newborn republic, but they took two more days to debate and to approve this declaration and announcement to the world of what they had done and the reasons why.

The Declaration and other great documents of our heritage remind me of the flying machines across the Mall in the new museum we opened yesterday. From the Spirit of St. Louis to the lunar orbital capsules, we see vehicles that enabled Americans to cross vast distances in space. In our archives and in our libraries, we find documents to transport us across centuries in time—back to Mount Sinai and the Sea of Galilee, to Runnymede, to the pitching cabin of the *Mayflower*, and to sweltering Philadelphia in midsummer 1776.

If we maneuver our time vehicle along to 1787, we see the chamber of Independence Hall, where the Constitution is being drafted under the stern eye of George Washington. Some other faces are familiar. Benjamin Franklin is there, of course, and Roger Sherman of Connecticut. Thomas Jefferson has gone to Paris. The quiet genius of this Convention is James Madison.

But Jefferson's principles are very much present. The Constitution, when it is done, will translate the great ideals of the Declaration into a legal mechanism for effective government where the unalienable rights of individual Americans are secure.

In grade school, we were taught to memorize the first and last parts of the Declaration. Nowadays, even many scholars skip over the long recitation of alleged abuses by King George III and his misguided ministers. But occasionally we ought to read them, because the injuries and invasions of individual rights listed there are the very excesses of government power which the Constitution, the Bill of Rights, and subsequent amendments were designed to prevent.

The familiar parts of the Declaration describe the positives of freedom; the dull part, the negatives. Not all the rights of free people—nor all the necessary powers of government—can be enumerated in one writing or for all time, as Madison and his colleagues made plain in the ninth and tenth amendments.

But the source of all unalienable rights, the proper purposes for which governments are instituted among men, and the reasons why free people should consent to an equitable ordering of their God-given freedom, have never been better stated than by Jefferson in our Declaration of Independence. Life, liberty, and the pursuit of happiness are cited as being among the most precious endowments of the Creator—but not the only ones.

Earlier, Jefferson wrote that "The God who gave us life gave us liberty at the same time." This better explains the bold assertion that "all Men are created equal" which Americans have debated for two centuries. We obviously are not equal in size, or wisdom, or strength, or fortune. But we are all born—having had nothing to say about it at all—and from the moment we have a life of our own, we have a liberty of our own, and we receive both in equal shares. We are all born free in the eyes of God.

That eternal truth is the great promise of the Declaration, but it certainly was not self-evident to most of mankind in 1776. I regret to say it is not universally accepted in 1976. Yet the American adventure not only proclaimed it, for two hundred years we have consistently sought to prove it true. The Declaration is the promise of freedom; the Constitution continuously seeks the fulfillment of freedom. The Constitution was created and continues—as its preamble states—"to secure the Blessings of Liberty to ourselves and our Posterity."

The great promise of the Declaration requires far more than the patriot sacrifices of the American Revolution, more than the legal stabilizer of the Constitution, more than Lincoln's successful answer to the question of whether a nation so conceived and so dedicated could long endure.

What does the Declaration declare?—that all human beings have certain rights as a gift from God; that these rights cannot lawfully be taken away from any man or woman by any human agency, monarchy, or democracy; that all governments derive their just powers from the people, who consent to be governed in order to secure their rights and to effect their safety and their happiness.

Thus, both rights and powers belong to the people; the rights equally apportioned to every individual, the powers to the people as a whole.

This November, the American people will, under the Constitution, again give their consent to be governed. This free and secret act should be a reaffirmation, by every eligible American, of the mutual pledges made two hundred years ago by John Hancock and the others whose untrembling signatures we can still make out.

Jefferson said that the future belongs to the living. We stand awed in the presence of these great charters not by their beauty, not by their antiquity, but because they belong to us. We return thanks that they have guided us safely through two centuries of national independence, but the excitement of this occasion is that they still work.

All around our nation's capital are priceless collections of America's great contributions to the world, but many of them are machines no longer used, inventions no longer needed, clothes no longer worn, books no longer read, songs no longer sung.

Not so the Constitution, which works for us daily, changing slowly to meet new needs; not so the Bill of Rights, which protects us day and night in the exercise of our fundamental freedoms—to pray, to publish, to speak as we please.

Above all stands the magnificent Declaration, still the fixed star of freedom for the United States of America.

Let each of us, in this year of our Bicentennial, join with those brave and farsighted Americans of 1776. Let us, here and now, mutually pledge to the ennobling and enduring principles of the Declaration our lives, our fortunes, and our sacred honor.

Let us do so, as they did, with firm reliance on the protection of divine Providence, that the future of this land that we love may be ever brighter for our children and for generations of Americans yet to be born.

APPENDIX

BIOGRAPHICAL NOTES

ALBERT, CARL (BERT) (1908-   ). Born, McAlester, Oklahoma; A.B., University of Oklahoma, 1931; Rhodes Scholar, B.A., Oxford University, 1933; B.C.L., 1934; LL.D., Oklahoma City University; admitted to Oklahoma bar, 1935; legal clerk, FHA, 1934-37; attorney-accountant, Sayre Oil Co., 1939-40; general law practice, 1938-47; member, US House of Representatives (Democrat, Oklahoma), 1947-76; Democrat Whip, 1955-62; majority leader, 1962-71; speaker, 1971-76; AUS, 1941-46; recipient, Bronze Star; member, Phi Beta Kappa; winner, National Oratorical Championship, 1928. (See also *Current Biography*: *June 1957*.)

BACON, WALLACE ALGER (1914-   ). Born, Bad Axe, Michigan; A.B., Albion College, 1935; M.A., University of Michigan, 1936; Ph.D., 1940; Lloyd Fellow, University of Michigan, 1940-41; instructor, Department of English, 1941-42, 1946-47; assistant professor of English and Speech, Northwestern University, 1947-50; associate professor, 1950-55; professor, 1955-   ; chairman, department of interpretation, School of Speech, 1947-   ; Rockefeller Foundation fellow, 1948-49; Ford Foundation fellow, 1954-55; Fulbright lecturer, University of Philippines, 1961-62; Fulbright-Hays lecturer, 1964-65; winner, Golden Anniversary Prize Fund (SCA), 1965, 1974; captain, AUS, 1942-46; Legion of Merit; author, *Savonarola*, 1950; (editor) *William Warner's Syrinx*, 1950; (coauthor) *Literature as Experience*, 1959; (coeditor) *Literature for Interpretation*, 1961; (coauthor) *The Art of Oral Interpretation*, 1965; *The Art of Interpretation*, 1966, 1972; (coauthor) *Spoken English*, 1962; *Oral Interpretation and Teaching of Literature in Secondary Schools*, 1974; president, Speech Communication Association, 1977; member, Phi Beta Kappa, Delta Sigma Rho, Theta Alpha Phi.

BOORSTIN, DANIEL JOSEPH (1914-   ). Born, Atlanta, Georgia; A.B., summa cum laude, Harvard University, 1934; B.A., first class honors, Rhodes scholar, Balliol College, Oxford University, 1936; B.C.L., 1937; J.S.D., Yale University, 1940; admitted, barrister-at-law, Inner Temple, 1937; instructor, history and literature, Harvard and Radcliffe, 1938-42; lecturer, legal history, Harvard Law School, 1939-42; admitted to Massachusetts bar, 1942; assistant professor of history, Swarthmore College, 1942-

44; assistant professor of history, University of Chicago, 1944-49; associate professor, 1949-56; professor, 1956-64; director, National Museum of History and Technology, Smithsonian Institution, 1969-73; senior librarian, 1973-75; Librarian of Congress, 1975- ; lecturer for US Department of State in Iran, India, Nepal, and elsewhere, 1959-60; Phi Beta Kappa; author, *The Mysterious Science of the Law*, 1941; *The Lost World of Thomas Jefferson*, 1948; *The Genius of American Politics*, 1953; *The Americans: The Colonial Experience*, 1958; *America and the Image of Europe*, 1960; *The Image, or What Happened to the American Dream*, 1962; *The Americans: The National Experience*, 1965; *The Landmark History of the American People*, 1968; *The Decline of Radicalism*, 1969; *The Sociology of the Absurd*, 1970; *The Americans: The Democratic Experience*, 1973 (Pulitzer prize, 1974); *Democracy and Its Discontents*, 1974; editor, *Chicago History of American Civilization* (27 vols.); *An American Primer*, 1966; *American Civilization*, 1972; American history editor, *Encyclopaedia Britannica*, 1951-55; articles and book reviews. (See also *Current Biography: September 1968*.)

BURGER, WARREN E (ARL) (1907-   ). Born, St. Paul, Minnesota; student, University of Minnesota, 1925-27; LL.B., magna cum laude, St. Paul College of Law (now William Mitchell College of Law); Doctor of Laws, 1931; honorary degrees, LL.D., William Mitchell College of Law, 1966, and New York Law School, 1976; admitted to Minnesota bar, 1931; faculty, William Mitchell College of Law, 1931-53; partner, Faricy, Burger, Moore & Costello (and predecessor firms), 1935-53; assistant attorney general in charge of Civil Division, US Department of Justice, 1953-56; judge of US Court of Appeals, District of Columbia, 1956-69; Chief Justice of the United States, 1969-   ; lecturer, American and European law schools; faculty, Appellate Judges Seminar, New York University Law School, 1958-   ; member and legal adviser to US delegation to International Labor Organization, Geneva, 1954; contributor to law journals and other publications. (See also *Current Biography: November 1969*.)

CARTER, JIMMY (JAMES EARL JR.) (1924-   ). Born, Plains, Georgia; student, Georgia Southwestern University, 1941-42; Georgia Institute of Technology, 1942-43; B.S., US Naval Academy, 1946; postgraduate instruction, nuclear physics, Union College, 1952; US Navy, 1947-53, advancing through grades to lieutenant commander; resigned 1953; farmer, warehouseman, 1953-77; served two terms in Georgia senate (Democrat), 1962-66 (voted most effective member); governor, 1971-74; chairman, Democratic National Campaign Committee, 1974; elected President, 1976; inaugurated, January 20, 1977; past president, Georgia Planning Association; first chairman, West Central Georgia Planning and Development Commission; former chairman, Sumter County Board of Education; district governor, Lions International; state chairman, March of Dimes; author, *Why Not the Best*, 1975. (See also *Current Biography: September 1971*.)

CROSBY, GLENN ARTHUR (1928-   ). Born, Hempfield Township, Pennsylvania; B.S., Waynesburg College, 1950; Ph.D., University of Washington, 1954; postdoctoral fellow, Florida State University, 1955-57; Fulbright fellow, University of Tübingen (West Germany), 1964; visiting professor of physics, University of Canterbury (New Zealand), 1974; professor, University of New Mexico, 1957-67; professor of chemistry and chemical physics, Washington State University, 1967-   ; named Outstanding Chemistry Teacher by Washington State Science Teachers' Association, 1975; author of over 60 publications in technical and scientific journals and 10 articles on chemical education.

FORD, GERALD RUDOLPH (1913-   ). Born, Omaha, Nebraska; B.A., University of Michigan, 1935; LL.B., Yale Law School, 1941; honorary degrees from several universities; admitted Michigan bar, 1941; private law practice, Grand Rapids, Michigan, 1941-49; member, US House of Representatives (Republican, Michigan), 1949-73; minority leader, 1965-73; appointed Vice President by President Nixon, confirmed by Congress, December 6, 1973; became president upon resignation of Nixon, August 9, 1974; President, 1974-77; lieutenant commander, US Navy, 1942-46; member, Delta Kappa Epsilon, Phi Delta Phi. (See also *Current Biography: November 1975*.)

GOODMAN, JULIAN (1922-   ). Born, Glasgow, Kentucky; A.B., George Washington University, 1948; A.B., Western Kentucky University, 1975; honorary degrees, William Jewell College (1967), University of Florida (1973); news writer, NBC, 1945-50; manager of news, Washington, D.C., 1950-59; director of news and public affairs, NBC network, 1959-61; vice president, NBC News, 1961-65; executive vice president, 1965; senior executive vice president, NBC, Inc., 1965; president, 1966-74; chairman of board, 1974-   ; AUS, 1943-45; National Association of Broadcasters' Distinguished Service Award, 1976; recipient of many other awards and offices in professional organizations.

HANNAH, JOHN ALFRED (1902-   ). Born, Grand Rapids, Michigan; B.S., Michigan State University, 1923; honorary degrees from over 25 colleges and universities; extension specialist,

200 Representative American Speeches

Michigan State University, 1923-33; management agent, Federal Hatchery Co-ordinating Commission (Kansas City, Mo.), 1933-35; secretary of board of trustees, Michigan State University, 1935-41; president, 1941-69; chairman, US Commission on Civil Rights, 1957-69; administrator, US Agency for International Development, 1969-73; consultant, 1973-74; deputy secretary general, 1974 UN World Food Conference, 1974; executive director, UN World Food Council, 1975-   ; member, numerous governmental and professional commissions; Phi Beta Kappa, Beta Sigma Sigma, Phi Eta Sigma, Alpha Phi Omega, Phi Kappa Phi, and Pi Kappa Delta.

HOLTZMAN, ELIZABETH (1941-   ). Born, Brooklyn, New York; B.A., magna cum laude, Radcliffe College, 1962; J.D., Harvard University, 1965; admitted to New York Bar, 1965; practiced law in New York City, 1965-72; assistant to mayor, New York City, 1967-70; member, US House of Representatives (Democrat, New York), 1973-   ; Phi Beta Kappa; recipient numerous awards. (See also Current Biography: November 1973.)

JORDAN, BARBARA C. (1936-   ). Born, Houston, Texas; B.A., magna cum laude, Texas Southern University, 1956; J.D., LL.B., Boston University, 1959; admitted to Massachusetts and Texas bars, 1959; administrative assistant to county judge, Harris County, Texas; member, Texas senate, 1967-72; US House of Representatives (Democrat, Texas), 1973-   ; member, board of directors, National Urban League, 1970-72; named one of Ten Most Influential Women in Texas, one of 100 Women in Touch With Our Time (Harper's Bazaar), Democratic Woman of the Year, Woman of the Year in Politics (Ladies Home Journal).

LINOWITZ, SOL MYRON (1913-   ). Born, Trenton, New Jersey; A.B., Hamilton College, 1935; J.D., Cornell University, 1938; honorary degrees from 23 colleges and universities; admitted to New York bar, 1938; assistant general counsel OPA, 1942-44; partner in Sutherland, Linowitz & Williams, 1946-58; Harris, Beach, Keating, Wilcox & Linowitz, 1958-66; senior partner, Coudert Brothers, 1969-   ; member of boards of numerous corporations; USNR, 1944-46; ambassador to OAS, 1966-69; chairman, National Urban Coalition, 1970-   ; member, Phi Beta Kappa, Phi Kappa Phi, Delta Sigma Rho, Order of Coif; author, This Troubled Urban World; contributor, professional journals.

McNAMARA, ROBERT STRANGE (1916-   ). Born, San Francisco, California; A.B., University of California, Berkeley, 1937; M.B.A., Harvard University, 1939; numerous honorary degrees;

with Price, Waterhouse, 1939; assistant professor, business administration, Harvard University, 1940-43; executive, Ford Motor Company, 1946-61; US Secretary of Defense, 1961-68; president, World Bank, 1968-   ; director, many public and private institutions; lieutenant colonel, USAAF, 1943-46; recipient, Legion of Merit, Medal of Freedom, D.S.M.; member, Phi Beta Kappa; author, *The Essence of Security*, 1968; *One Hundred Countries, Two Billion People*, 1973. (See also *Current Biography: September 1961.*)

MOORE, PAUL JR. (1919-   ). Born, Morristown, New Jersey; B.A., Yale University, 1941; S.T.B., General Theological Seminary (New York City), 1949; honorary degrees, 1960, 1964; member of team ministry, Grace Church, Jersey City, 1949-57; dean, Christ Church Cathedral, Indianapolis, 1957-64; suffragan bishop, Washington, D.C., 1964-70; bishop coadjuter, diocese of New York, 1970-72; bishop, 1972-   ; served to captain, USMCR, 1941-45; recipient, Navy Cross, Silver Star, Purple Heart; member, Legal Defense Fund, NAACP, 1956-   ; National Recreation Association, 1956-   ; urban division, National Council of the Episcopal Church, 1955-   ; urban advisory committee, 1962-   ; trustee, General Theological Seminary, 1957-   ; fellow, Yale Corporation, 1964-   ; author, *The Church Reclaims the City*, 1970 (2d ed.); contributed chapters to *Viewpoints, Some Aspects of Anglican Thinking*, 1959 and *On the Battlelines*, 1964. (See also *Current Biography: January 1967.*)

NORTON, ELEANOR HOLMES (1937-   ). Born, Washington, D.C.; B.A., Antioch College, 1960; M.A., Yale University, 1963; LL.B., 1964; five honorary degrees, 1969-75; law clerk to Federal Judge A. Leon Higginbotham, 3d Circuit, 1964-65; assistant legal director, American Civil Liberties Union, 1965-70; chairman, New York City Commission on Human Rights, 1970-77; executive assistant, Mayor John V. Lindsay (New York), 1971-73; head, Equal Employment Opportunity Commission, 1977-   ; author (with Babcock, Freeman, and Ross), *Sex Discrimination*, 1975; named as one of 200 Rising Leaders Under 45, *Time*, July 17, 1974. (See also *Current Biography: November 1976.*)

ROCKEFELLER, NELSON A. (1908-   ). Born, Bar Harbor, Maine; B.A., Dartmouth College, 1930; director, Rockefeller Center, Inc., 1931-58; president, 1938-45, chairman, 1945-53, 1956-58; coordinator, Office of Inter-American Affairs, 1940-44; assistant Secretary of State for American Republic Affairs, 1944-45; chairman, International Development Board (Point 4 program), 1950-51; under secretary, US Department of Health, Education, and Welfare, 1953-54; special assistant to President Eisenhower, 1954-55; governor of New York, 1959-73; Vice President of the United States, 1974-77; member, Phi Beta Kappa; author, *The Future of Federalism*, 1962; *Unity, Freedom, and Peace*, 1968; *Our Environment Can Be Saved*, 1970. (See also *Current Biography: March 1951*.)

SAYRE, FRANCIS BOWLES JR. (1915-   ). Born, Washington, D.C.; A.B., cum laude, Williams College, 1937; B.D., Episcopal Theological School (Cambridge, Mass.), 1940; eight honorary degrees, 1956-73; ordained to ministry, 1940; assistant minister, Christ Church (Cambridge, Mass.), 1940-42; chaplain, diocese of Ohio, Cleveland, 1946-51; rector, St. Paul Church, East Cleveland, Ohio, 1947-51; dean, Washington Cathedral, 1951-   ; chaplain, USNR, 1942-46. (See also *Current Biography: December 1956*.)

STENDAHL, KRISTER (1921-   ). Born, Stockholm, Sweden; Th.D., Uppsala University, Sweden, 1954; ordained, Church of Sweden, 1944; assistant pastor, diocese of Stockholm, 1944-46; chaplain, Uppsala University, 1948-50; instructor, 1951-54; docent, 1954; assistant professor, Divinity School, Harvard University, 1954-56; associate professor, 1956-58; John H. Morison Professor of New Testament Studies, 1958-63; Frothingham Professor of Biblical Studies, 1963-68; dean, Divinity School, John Lord O'Brian Professor of Divinity, 1968-   ; Guggenheim fellow, 1951, 1974; fellow, American Academy of Arts and Sciences; author, *The School of St. Matthew and Its Use of the Old Testament*, 1968 (2d ed.); *The Bible and the Role of Women*, 1966; *Holy Week*, 1974; *Paul Among Jews and Gentiles*, 1976; editor, *The Scrolls and the New Testament*, 1957; numerous articles and essays in Swedish, German, and American journals and encyclopedias.

VANCE, CYRUS ROBERTS (1917-   ). Born, Clarksburg, West Virginia; B.A., Yale University, 1939; LL.B., 1942; five honorary degrees, 1963-71; admitted to New York Bar, 1947; US Supreme Court bar, 1960; assistant to president, Mead Corporation, 1946-47; with Simpson Thacher & Bartlett, New York City, 1947-56; partner, 1956-61; general counsel, US Department of Defense, 1961-62; US Secretary of Army, 1962-63; deputy Secretary of Defense, 1964-67; special representative of President: Cyprus, 1967; Korea, 1968; US Negotiator Paris Peace Conference on Vietnam, 1968-69; US Secretary of State, 1977-   ; director, trustee, many organizations; USNR, 1942-46; recipient, Medal of Freedom, 1969. (See also *Current Biography: December 1962*.)

WALTERS, BARBARA (1931-   ). Born, Boston, Massachusetts; B.A., Sarah Lawrence College, 1953; honorary degrees, Ohio State University and Marymount College, 1975; former writer-producer, WNBC-TV and CBS-TV; joined ABC as anchor woman, 1976-   ; Emmy award, National Academy of TV Arts and Sciences, 1975; named one of 100 Women of Accomplishment (*Harper's Bazaar*), 1967, 1971; one of America's 75 Most Important Women (*Ladies Home Journal*) 1970; Woman of the Year in Communications, 1974; one of 200 Leaders of the Future (*Time*), 1974; author, *How to Talk With Practically Anybody About Practically Anything*, 1970; contributor, *Good Housekeeping, Family Weekly, Reader's Digest*. (See also *Current Biography: February 1971*.)

CUMULATIVE AUTHOR INDEX

1970-1971—1976-1977

A cumulative author index to the volumes of REPRESENTATIVE AMERICAN SPEECHES for the years 1937-1938 through 1959-1960 appears in the 1959-1960 volume and for the years 1960-1961 through 1969-1970 in the 1969-1970 volume.

Abzug, B. S. 1971-72, 37-48, A new kind of southern strategy

Aiken, G. D. 1973-74, 66-73, Either impeach . . . or get off his back

Albert, Carl. 1976-77, 188-90, Bicentennial of American independence

Andrus, C. D. 1970-71, 137-41, The inaugural address

Bacon, W. A. 1976-77, 174-80, Language and the lived world

Barger, R. N. 1973-74, 177-85, Theology and amnesty

Billington, R. A. 1975-76, 176-92, Cowboys, Indians, and the land of promise: the world image of the American frontier

Boorstin, D. J. 1976-77, 138-48, Beginnings

Brewster, Kingman Jr. 1972-73, 176-93, The decade of short-cuts

Brooke, E. W. 1973-74, 74-86, Responsibilities inherent in a constitutional democracy

Burger, W. E. 1970-71, 13-28, State of the judiciary; 1976-77, 186-8, Bicentennial of American independence

Burke, Y. B. 1974-75, 143-7, "Aspirations . . . unrequited"

Butz, E. L. 1974-75, 81-8, Feast or famine: the key to peace

Carter, Jimmy. 1970-71, 142-6, Inauguration address; 1976-77, 18-23, Inaugural address; 1976-77, 30-51, The third presidential debate; 1976-77, 117-26, Energy problems

Cheek, J. E. 1970-71, 131-5, A promise made, a promise to keep: Whitney Young and the nation

Chisholm, Shirley. 1971-72, 27-36, Economic injustice in America today; 1972-73, 79-85, Women in politics

Church, Frank. 1970-71, 49-62, Foreign policy and the generation gap; 1975-76, 124-32, Rediscovering America

Clifford, C. M. 1972-73, 109-18, "We must renew our confidence"

Cole, E. N. 1971-72, 93-9, Two myths and a paradox

Cornish, D. T. 1975-76, 207-16, A warrior against fate

Cox, Archibald. 1973-74, 49-65, Creativity in law and government

Crosby, G. A. 1976-77, 156-67, The uses of adversity

Dabney, Virginius. 1974-75, 168-80, Facts and the Founding Fathers

Dennis, D. W. 1974-75, 35-42, Hearings on articles of impeachment by the Committee on the Judiciary of the House of Representatives: for the defense

Dubos, R. J. 1972-73, 149-60, Humanizing the earth

Edwards, George. 1971-72, 101-10, Murder and gun control

Eilberg, Joshua. 1974-75, 25-9, Hearings on articles of impeachment by the Committee on the Judiciary of the House of Representatives: for the prosecution

Elson, E. L. R. 1971-72, 151-60, Freaks for Jesus' sake

Everheart, W. E. 1975-76, 27-33, We hold these truths

Fawcett, N. G. 1970-71, 106-14, Direction for destiny

Flowers, Walter. 1974-75, 30-4, Hearings on articles of impeachment by the Committee on the Judiciary of the House of Representatives: undecided

Ford, G. R. 1973-74, 193, Acceptance speech; 1974-75, 50-3, First presidential address; 1975-76, 133-51, Presidential remarks with question-and-answer session; 1976-77, 30-51, The third presidential debate; 1976-77, 192-6, Bicentennial of American independence

Fulbright, J. W. 1974-75, 109-16, "The neglect of the song"

Galbraith, J. K. 1975-76, 78-87, On history, political economy, and Vietnam

Gallagher, Wes. 1973-74, 132-40, "Free just free"

Gardner, J. W. 1972-73, 119-31, Education; 1974-75, 158-67, People power

Goodman, Julian, 1976-77, 52-60, Broadcast journalism: serving the democratic process

Goodman, S. J. 1973-74, 160-75, Raising the fallen image of business

Graham, Billy. 1975-76, 34-47, Our Bicentennial

Hannah, J. A. 1976-77, 103-16, Meeting world food needs

Harris, J. G. 1971-72, 143-50, The prayer amendment

Hartzog, G. B. Jr. 1972-73, 194-9, Finding America

Hatfield, M. O. 1972-73, 91-3, Reconciliation and peace; 1973-74, 105-18, The energy crisis; 1974-75, 89-96, Global interdependence: "Life, liberty, and the pursuit of happiness" in today's world

Hesburgh, T. M. 1970-71, 85-93, Higher education begins the seventies

Holtzman, Elizabeth. 1976-77, 80-90, Women and equality under the law

Horner, M. S. 1972-73, 184-93, Opportunity for educational innovation

Howard, J. A. 1970-71, 94-105, The innovation mirage; 1975-76, 9-26, Our sacred honor

Howe, Harold II. 1972-73, 161-75, Public education for a humane society

Hutchins, R. M. 1971-72, 161-71, The institutional illusion; 1974-75, 117-26, All our institutions are in disarray

James, Daniel Jr. 1974-75, 135-42, "Given time we'll get it together"

Jeffrey, R. C. 1973-74, 119-31, Ethics in public discourse

Johnson, L. B. 1972-73, 138-48, As the days dwindle down

Jordan, B. C. 1974-75, 19-24, Hearings on articles of impeachment by the Committee on the Judiciary of the House of Representatives: an introduction; 1976-77, 11-17, Keynote address

Jordan, V. E. Jr. 1971-72, 49-58, Survival; 1972-73, 39-49, Blacks and the Nixon Administration: the next four years; 1975-76, 88-101, Unfinished business

Keeler, W. W. 1971-72, 74-7, Inaugural address of the chief of the Cherokees

Kelley, C. M. 1975-76, 117-23, Terrorism, the ultimate evil

Kennedy, E. M. 1971-72, 68-73, La Raza and the law

Kissinger, H. A. 1973-74, 87-95, Statement to the Senate Foreign Relations Committee; 1974-75, 62-80, Address before the World Food Conference; 1975-76, 48-64, America's permanent interests

Krug, J. F. 1975-76, 193-206, In defense of liberty: extremism and other vices

Linowitz, S. M. 1976-77, 149-55, "Let candles be brought"

McBath, J. H. 1974-75, 127-34, The vital university

McGill, W. J. 1971-72, 182-97, The public challenge and the campus response

McGovern, G. S. 1972-73, 22-38, American politics: a personal view

McNamara, R. S. 1976-77, 91-102, Searching for new solutions to poverty

Marcus, Stanley. 1975-76, 152-65, Can free enterprise survive success?

Mathias, C. M. Jr. 1972-73, 60-3, Truth in government

Mead, Margaret. 1973-74, 97-104, The planetary crisis and the challenge to scientists

Mink, P. T. 1971-72, 59-67, Seeking a link with the past

Moore, Paul Jr. 1976-77, 24-9, A biblical faith for a President

Moos, M. C. 1973-74, 148-59, Restoring the tidemarks of trust

Moynihan, D. P. 1970-71, 29-36, The middle of the journey; 1975-76, 65-77, Worldwide amnesty for political prisoners

Murphy, P. V. 1970-71, 122-9, What the police expect of the citizenry

Nader, Ralph. 1971-72, 79-92, Meet the Press

Nelson, G. A. 1973-74, 188, Against the nomination of Gerald R. Ford [as Vice President]

Nixon, R. M. 1970-71, 37-48, Remarks at the White House Conference on Children; 1971-72, 13-26, State of the Union message; 1972-73, 15-21, Second inaugural address; 1972-73, 50-9, The Watergate case; 1973-74, 24-39, Press conference; 1974-75, 43-9, Speech of resignation

Norton, E. H. 1976-77, 65-79, In pursuit of equality in academe: new themes and dissonant chords

Parson, M. J. 1975-76, 166-75, Idealism, what's wrong with it?

Peden, William. 1972-73, 94-100, Is Thomas Jefferson relevant?

Percy, C. H. 1973-74, 189-92, For the nomination of Gerald R. Ford [as Vice President]

Peterson, Martha. 1970-71, 73-84, In these present crises

Powell, L. F. Jr. 1972-73, 101-8, The eroding authority

Richardson, E. L. 1973-74, 13-23, Vulnerability and vigilance

Rockefeller, N. A. 1976-77, 190-2, Bicentennial of American independence

Rogers, W. P. 1974-75, 54-61, A brief assessment of where we stand today

Ruckelshaus, Jill. 1972-73, 65-78, Meet the Press

Ruckelshaus, W. D. 1971-72, 125-32, The environment revolution

Rusk, Dean. 1972-73, 132-7, Eulogy of Lyndon Baines Johnson

Sargent, F. W. 1973-74, 141-7, The computer and civil liberties

Sawhill, J. C. 1975-76, 102-16, Energy and the job market

Sayre, F. B. Jr. 1976-77, 181-4, The tall ships

Schlesinger, Arthur Jr. 1971-72, 133-41. Roosevelt's place in history

Schroeder, Patricia. 1972-73, 86-9, You can do it

Spencer, S. R. Jr. 1971-72, 172-81, A call for new missionaries

Steinem, Gloria. 1972-73, 65-78, Meet the Press

Stendahl, Krister. 1976-77, 168-73, "Faith that enlivens the mind"

Stewart, Potter. 1974-75, 97-108, Or of the press

Trotter, V. Y. 1974-75, 148-57, A shift in the balance

Vance, Cyrus. 1976-77, 127-37, Human rights and the foreign policy

Von Braun, Wernher. 1971-72, 111-24, Earth benefits from space and space technology

Walker, H. B. 1970-71, 63-71, The future of the past

Walters, Barbara. 1976-77, 31-51, The third presidential debate [moderator's introductory remarks and closing statement]

Watson, T. J. Jr. 1970-71, 115-21, Medical care

Weicker, L. P. Jr. 1973-74, 40-7, The Watergate investigation; 1976-77, 61-4, Televised debates

DATE DUE

GAYLORD			PRINTED IN U.S.A.